MAK (

MW00910475

2/09

General Information:
MAK Center for Art and Architecture, L.A. at the Schindler House
835 North Kings Road
West Hollywood, CA 90069-5409
phone (213) 651-1510
fax (213) 651-2340

Directions: The Schindler House is located four blocks east of La Cienega and two blocks north of Melrose, on the west side of the street, behind the row of bamboo plants.

Hours:
Wednesday through Sunday, 11:00 am to 6:00 pm
Closed Monday and Tuesday

Guided Tours:
Regular guided tours are available on weekends only.
To arrange for group tours at other times, please call (213) 651-1510.

Note: Photography of the house and its grounds is permitted during the center's open hours.

Admission:
$5 for adults, seniors, or students. Free to members of the Friends of the Schindler House and children under 18.

Admission free on Schindler's birthday, September 10, on International Museum Day, May 24, and on
December 1, "A Day Without Art."

Membership:
Membership in the Friends of the Schindler House is $ 40.00 per year for adults and $ 20.00 for students.

Mackey Apartments:
1137 South Cochran Avenue
Los Angeles, CA 90019
Open to the public only during special events or by appointment, call (213) 651-1510.

Directions: The Mackey Apartments are located six blocks west of La Brea, between Olympic and San Vincente Boulevards.

MAK Center for Art and Architecture
R.M. Schindler

Edited by Peter Noever
for MAK, Vienna,
and
MAK Center for Art and Architecture, Los Angeles

Prestel
Munich · New York

MAK Center for Art and Architecture, L.A.

In the spirit of Rudolf M. Schindler, the experimental architect and social utopian, the MAK Center for Art and Architecture, L.A., seeks out and supports projects/ideas which break the disciplinary boundaries between the fields of art and architecture. It examines what is shared and what is distinct in the concepts and methods of artists and architects operating within spatial categories. Through its programs, MAK Center, L.A. acts as a "think tank" for current issues in art and architecture, allowing for explorations of the practical and theoretical aspects, engaging the center's places, spaces, and histories. MAK Center, L.A. has a year-round schedule of exhibitions, symposiums, lectures, performances, workshops, and publications, and hosts a residency program for visiting artists and architects. It has also joined the Friends of the Schindler House (FOSH) in its mission to preserve, promote, and allow public access to the Schindler House.

Schindler House (R.M. Schindler, 1921-22)

Most MAK Center, L.A. programs are presented in Rudolf M. Schindler's residence and studio which, since 1994, is in the process of being carefully restored and adapted for public use. The house is an experimental model of Schindler's architecture and his most mature and prototypical design. Throughout the 1920s and 30s, it was the center of Los Angeles' avant-garde intellectual community. It was home to architect Richard Neutra, historian Charles Jenks, and the artists John Cage and Edward Weston. Now, once again, it is a focus point for L. A.'s artistic community.

MAK Center Bookstore

The bookstore located in the Schindler House offers catalogs produced by the MAK Center, L.A. and MAK-Austrian Museum of Applied Arts, Vienna, as well as related art and architecture publications. It is open during the center's regular hours.

Pearl M. Mackey Apartments (R. M. Schindler 1939)

Located just a few miles from the Schindler House, the four-unit apartment house was completely restored in 1994. The Mackey House possesses typical Schindler characteristics: compact apartment layout, exceptional incorporation of natural light, built-in furniture, variable ceiling levels, and private outdoor gardens or mini-balconies. The apartments are a noteworthy example of one of Schindler's only single, multiple-unit buildings and of his later designs.

Artists and Architects-in-Residence Program

The Mackey Apartments houses the MAK Center, L.A.'s Artists and Architects-in-Residence Program designed for visiting European artists and students of architecture. Six-month residencies are offered for two artists and two architecture students, during which time they each conceptualize, complete, and present a project.

MAK Center Archives

Housed within the Mackey Apartments, the MAK Center Archives focus on experimental art and architecture and on the architecture of Rudolf Schindler. They include a systematic compilation of projects, buildings, and works of art which demarcate the fields of art and architecture, as well as research material, including publications, exhibitions, and scholarly writings. The archive also documents and registers all exhibitions, installations, symposiums, performances, projects, and special events initiated by MAK Center, L.A. or by the artists or architects in residence at the Mackey Apartments. The archives will be accessible to the public and researchers (also through a World Wide Web page on Internet) in 1997.

Contents

Rudi, why aren´t you coming back? Mimi (April 1920)
Letter to R.M. Schindler from Schindler Archives, Santa Barbara.
After leaving Vienna in 1914, R.M. Schindler never returned to Austria.

The Question is the Question
The spirit of R.M. Schindler

Since the current context of activities in art represents a permanent exchange between fields of force and unstable states of motion, and not a fixed and static system of reference, the function of institutions in that context must also be redefined.

For, if an institution is to operate within this open system of multiple and swiftly changing references, it must face the challenge to question its own basis of existence. From a cultural stronghold irrevocably anchored in space and time, in other words, rooted in its own history and deriving therefrom in linear succession, it must become a mobile impulsor, a pole that functions simultaneously as a transmitter and receiver in a network of international links. Only if it is prepared to include its own identity in such processes of transformation can it fulfil the kind of role that is truly relevant to the present:

Envelope from letter, April 1920

a role in which it poses the right questions at the right time and thereby triggers further questions; a role that has freed it from the necessity for physical and historically legitimized presence so as to define itself as an ideal link transcending frontiers.

The MAK Schindler initiative, with all its multifarious and still far from foreseeable activities and strategies, feels primarily committed to a memory which is less to be preserved than built upon; to a vision of openness and a spirit of daring innovation which few have better personified than Rudolf Schindler. This, however, entails that memory should divorce itself from a hidebound, museological attitude so as to become part of that system of fields of force in which significant processes can permanently be set in motion.

Occupying the ideal center of the commitment that has forged a renewed frontier-transcending link between Vienna and Los Angeles are innovations, new trends, and interdisciplinary developments that pursue spatial structures and conceptual and experimental first endeavors. Schindler's radicality, both in his work and throughout his life, which were inextricably entwined, is the MAK initiative's sole and fundamental guideline.

Self-contained disciplinary discourse must be abandoned in favor of comprehensive initiatives and modes of thinking which alone can render it possible to carry out interdisciplinary projects. Interfaces, hybrid categories, and open systems are systematically encouraged by means of symposia, scientific publications, conferences, and commissioned works, the long-term outcome being globally defined projects. The viewpoint is subjective, the method experimental, the mode of procedure non-museological, ahistorical, non-systematic, and discursive. The Center being a think tank, research institute, and laboratory of thinking, it can only impart stimuli and address subjects and questions relating to art and architecture in an open, spontaneous, and flexible manner.

The aim is to create spaces and areas where new dimensions can be freely and openly subjected to artistic inquiry. The MAK Center is altogether consistent in regarding itself as a source of developments and opportunities, not of finished and final results. Its task is to create the conditions in which new projects and ideas can arise, whether by means of the artists and architects-in-residence program or through a more global understanding of what an exchange between Vienna and Los Angeles can signify in the present context.

The founding of the MAK Center for Art and Architecture is intended to forge links and create organizational structures that are, on the one hand, loose and wide-meshed enough to do justice to Schindler's pioneering spirit, and, on the other, concrete and specific enough purposefully to initiate actual interventions here and now.

The interaction of art and architecture, a process basic to the 20th century and exemplified with particular clarity by Schindler's work, points the way to a future in which the boundaries between different disciplines will be eliminated in the same way as national, hierarchical, or static dogmatisms. If the MAK Center has been founded under the auspices of internationalism and a wholehearted readiness to experiment, this means that it feels a sense of duty to this very future. It will only be possible, I believe, to meet these demands through a multiplicity of new ideas and activities if we succeed in asking the right question at the right time. This appears to be the sole fundamental point in actually tackling new paths to turn an experimental way of thinking into reality.

Peter Noever

Schindler House

Schindler House, 1995

R.M. Schindler´s room, 1995

Schindler House, rear view, 1995

View into the garden from R.M. Schindler´s room, 1995

11

The Present Position
The MAK Center for Art and Architecture, Los Angeles

Daniela Zyman

R.M. Schindler
at construction site 1940

Rudolf M. Schindler's complex and exceptional œuvre is one of the focal and neuralgic points of reference in the framing of a museological strategy devoted to present requirements. It has become the central challenge and commitment of the Rudolf M. Schindler Architectural Initiative called into being in 1991 by the MAK Austrian Museum of Applied Arts. In his over 100 projects and buildings, Schindler experimented with spatial structures and architectural principles that have retained their relevance and radicality to this day, as witnessed in statements by leading contemporary architects. As a social utopian and an experimental architect, he evolved ideal designs and exemplary schemes in regard to spatial planning, building technology and social housing that pioneered a new approach to architecture. His own West Hollywood residence and studio, built in 1921-22 is the purest and most radical manifestation of his uncompromising originality.

In adopting a firmly contemporary direction and encouraging artists and architects who pursue experimental projects and working methods, the MAK Center for Art and Architecture has not only made experimentation its defining principle but places it, as an ideal commitment, in the forefront of its activities. In this connection, its point of departure is intended to be the interface between art and architecture; that is the point at which concepts and working methods of artists and architects who operate with spatial categories overlap and conflict. It seeks to initiate and further projects and activities to demarcate a basic procedural structure productive on an open working environment not restricted by self-contained disciplines and methods.

These activities are taking place at two locations in Los Angeles. The Pearl M. Mackey House (1939) has been purchased by the Republic of Austria to accommodate artists and architects in residence—an acquisition that established Austria's first permanent residence for artists abroad and the first scholarship program in Los Angeles. The MAK Center's second base is the architect's own former residence, the Schindler House on Kings Road in West Hollywood, only a few miles from the Mackey House.

From Vienna to Los Angeles
A (Possible) Historical Overview

Schindler moved away from the capital of the Austro-Hungarian Empire in 1914, shortly before the outbreak of the First World War. Then twenty-six years old, he left Vienna to (re)discover the New World and the fascination that had taken Adolf Loos to Chicago and New York before the turn of the century. In so doing, he unwittingly and unintentionally coincided with the start of an interaction that was to exert a fundamental influence on the 20th century—one whose routes and connections extended from Prague, Brno, Vienna, Chicago, and New York to the far west of the United States. As a "modern" architect, Schindler turned his back on the Old World to seek a way to realize his vision of spatial architecture. "I believe that climate and character, in company with a further genuine development of spatial architecture, will make Southern California the cradle of a new form of architectural expression."

Like Schindler, a whole series of Austrian architects—Victor Gruen, Frederick Kiesler, Richard Neutra, Bernard Rudofsky, and Josef Urban, to name but a few—obeyed the call of the new that promised to supersede Europe as the center of culture and art. The old continent, which not only stagnated but steadily regressed after 1918, was threatened with destruction by itself, its structures, its incapacity for genuine renewal, and was to disintegrate completely in 1933. We cannot now say for certain whether Schindler was guided by a premonition, or whether it was simply in his nature to seek what was different, unexplored, and original.

But Schindler also stood on the threshold of an age when "new" America, still partly crude, uncultivated, and embodied in Wright's romantically archaic ideas, contrasting with its industrial architecture and the daring beauty of its skyscrapers, seemed more desirable and challenging than Europe's refined guiding principles and restrictive formalisms, and when all this suggested that it would be worthwhile to journey afar and accept the risk of non-arrival. Being a visionary, not a dreamer, Schindler was thoroughly alive to what he was embarking on and what he was after. "If I am to speak of 'American architecture', " he wrote to Richard Neutra in 1920-21, "I'm bound to say, right away, that no such thing yet exists. There are a few rudiments, but architecture has never truly become wedded to America."

His ultimate destination, after intermediate but decisive stops in Chicago, where he worked first in the studio of Ottenheimer, Stern and Reichert, and later for Frank Lloyd Wright in Chicago and at Taliesin, near the Grand Canyon, was Los Angeles. In deciding to settle there, Schindler once more paralleled an influential movement and became part of the visionary tendency which, albeit spearheaded by other art forms, had chosen California as a "dreamland": the Hollywood of the film industry. Schindler's arrival coincided almost exactly with this first motion picture influx. This may latently have accounted for his decisions to locate his first building—the house, studio and materialized architectural vision whose radicality and originality of design he may never again have surpassed—in West Hollywood, which in the early 1920s was situated amid a lonely wasteland but also in immediate proximity to the Hollywood of the stars.

From 1922 onwards, quite in keeping with the lifestyle of the dream factory, the Kings Road house became a cultural phenomenon, the home base where Schindler surrounded himself with artists, intellectuals, and architects, cultivated an extravagant, unconventional life style, and finally abandoned his desire to return to Europe. The Schindler House was as much an architectural statement as a vision of "communal living", of a modern social experiment. Schindler's house broke with all the traditional rules of interior layout, of "homeliness", of division into private and public spaces and indoor and outdoor areas. It was conceived as a social camp fire: the rooms formed individual studio rooms for each of the occupants, who originally numbered four; the kitchen was designed as a central, functional utility room; the sleeping area on the roof—the "sleeping baskets"—made it possible to sleep in the open air; and the courts and terraces reserved for social functions were equipped with outdoor fireplaces and could thus, if covered over, be used as inner rooms. The house became a center of attraction whose fame and fascination extended to Europe.

Schindler was an experimenter with an unerring sense of the new age's inherent opportunities for overcoming existing limitations, whether of the Wagner school, of Wright's architecture, of the international style, or of his collaboration with Richard Neutra, which was lacking in flexibility. He was devoted to freedom, to originality, and a loner's "differentness" that was seldom understood and became an impediment to him, certainly from the professional aspect. In Frank Lloyd Wright's opinion he was "an incorrigible bohemian", in that of Philip Johnson, "an artiste".

From left to right: R.M. Schindler, Pauline Schindler, Sophie Gibling, Edmund Gibling holding Mark Schindler, Dorothy Gibling at the rear, summer 1923

The MAK Schindler Initiative, Los Angeles

The MAK involvement with Schindler was initiated by one of the first exhibitions to be held at the new MAK in 1986 "R.M. Schindler, Architect, 1887–1953,"[1] the first time his life's work had ever been shown in Austria. This important exhibition disclosed how little known the architect's buildings were, not only in his native land but internationally as well. In the winter of 1991, when MAK began to seek out traces of Schindler's work in and around Los Angeles, it became clear how little this situation had changed. His trail led to La Jolla, to the pueblo built in 1923/25 and half destroyed by fire, possibly because it was in the

Exhibition poster, MAK 1986

way of some property speculators; to the architect's home and studio, the house on Kings Road; to Silverlake, where some of his once "elegant" villas can still be discovered in part; and to Newparts Beach, where the Lovell Beach House icon has been disfigured by additions of a later date. As research progressed, this encounter with Schindler in Los Angeles developed to an increasing extent into a "commitment" to the voluntary exile and, thus, into an opportunity for Austria, the country that had lost and displaced so many thousands of its intellectual and creative community. It was this that prompted the basic and primary decision to take an initiative that might not only encourage the preservation of Schindler's architecture but—even more importantly, perhaps—perpetuate his vision in the interests of further progress and the promotion and shaping of today's art and architecture. California, which had steadily evolved during the 1970s and 1980s into a new center of artistic and architectural endeavor, seemed to view its own history with equal reservations.

The MAK Schindler Initiative, which was based on a feasibility study[2] and enjoyed the dedicated cooperation of the Republic of Austria, very soon assumed concrete shape. A revival of the relations between Vienna and Los Angeles, the extension of the now purely topographical boundaries that impose no binding conditions on art and architecture, the resuscitation of the Schindler House that used to be a center for L.A.'s avant-garde intellectual community in the 1920s and 1930s, and active exchanges effected by means of an art and architecture residency program at the Mackey House—such were the foundation stones of the far-reaching plan that was put into effect, step by step, between 1994 and 1996. The key-points in its implementation were as follows: cooperation with the Friends of the Schindler House (August 1994); purchase of the Mackey Apartment House (June 1995); inauguration of the artists program (October 1995), and inception of activities at the MAK Center (April 1996).

The Schindler House
and the Friends of the Schindler House

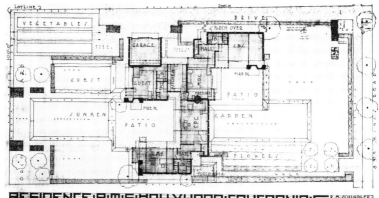

Floor plan of the Schindler House, 1922

Since 1980, when it was acquired from Pauline Schindler's estate by the Friends of the Schindler House, a non-profit organisation dedicated to preserving the house, the Schindler House on Kings Road has been a historic house museum. Being one of the few historic landmarks in the newly-established town of West Hollywood, it was progressively restored and, more especially, divested of Pauline's aesthetic and practical alterations which she added after Schindler's death in 1953. This renovation work was aimed at restoring the house and the gardens—which Schindler planned with extreme care but never completed—to their original condition in 1922. Work on the house proved not only extremely difficult, but costly and labor-intensive. It was built in 1921-22 as a very low-budget, quasi-homemade project using inexpensive and readily available materials, so its defects were omnipresent: water damage occasioned by permeable roof openings and clerestory windows; crumbling concrete structures; materials in constant need of replacement, e.g. canvas doors, internal and external "Insulite" panels, silk screens, and paper shades; rusting concrete reinforcements, deteriorating timber members. The repair and maintenance of the house and gardens were, and continue to be, a battle with the shortcomings in material and planning that nonetheless constitute the building's unique aesthetic charm and uncommonly stimulating and fragile appearance.

View into Clyde Chace's room, 1995

Schindler House, north sleeping porch, 1995

Thanks to the indefatigable work and commitment of FOSH, the Schindler House has not only been preserved from further decay but has become something of a place of pilgrimage for artists and architects. For years, a succession of architects and artists braved its considerable inconveniences in order to live and work in the tiny guest apartment. Architects of international repute visited and revered the Schindler House and followed its author's architectural lead, yet the building was underrated and often misunderstood within its own community.

In 1991, when MAK evinced a definite interest in completing the restoration work and launching an active program for the promotion of art and architecture, it laid the foundations of a collaboration by the two institutions which was not formalized until 1994. The cooperation within the framework of the MAK Center for Art and Architecture, a very exceptional and, for Austria, unprecedented undertaking, is based on the combined efforts and harmonized interests of FOSH and MAK.

The MAK-Austrian Museum of Applied Arts, Vienna, and the MAK Center for Art and Architecture, L.A.

MAK, Vienna, Stubenring entrance

Following Peter Noever's appointment as director of MAK and its consequent reorientation, MAK has since 1986 begun to define an exhibition and museum program which, in addition to the research and scientific evaluation of the traditional collection of arts and craft and applied art, has made it a central task to address the art, architecture, and design of today. Within the general context of newly defined museum work, the exploration of new developments, the study of interfaces (in traditional works as well), and the confrontation with the results and perspectives of contemporary artistic trends became not only a stimulating and rewarding focal point but a challenge to submit one's own positions to critical scrutiny. This has initiated a process aimed at gradually resolving the conflict between "applied" and "fine" art so as to inaugurate an often controversial process of exchange conducted primarily by artists, philosophers, architects, and scientists.

MAK, Vienna, Permanent Collection Jugendstil Historicism, installed by Barbara Bloom, 1993

The activities in Los Angeles are a continuation and extension of the museological strategies developed within MAK. Their main themes are internationalism, a clear dedication to experimentation, the testing of new ideas, and the promotion of art and architecture. The MAK Center for Art and Architecture, which is structurally linked to the history of the museum and its annexes, is thus, from the organizational aspect, a branch of MAK. Above all, though, it represents a strategic step towards implementing the institution's overall plan and vision. The obligation to concern itself with contemporary art and architecture within the framework of its own history is being developed into an independent project by establishing an international experimental research center in Los Angeles. In the main, however, the Schindler initiative should be seen as a stimulating factor whose purpose is to initiate trend-setting activities and innovations, thereby functioning as an instigator of dialogues in the field of contemporary art and architecture.

The aims of the MAK Center are promotive of concentration on theoretical and communicative work. Only occasional exhibitions are planned, primarily in order to display the results of the Center's activities and the processes it has initiated. The said activities embrace lectures, seminars, collections of material, workshops, debates, and the dissemination of information by means of small, selective publications and other media. It is further intended that new approaches to art and architecture be systematically fostered by basic scientific activity and documentation in the form of data bases and photographic archives relating to persons and projects. In this respect, the prime requirements are cooperation with local universities, international artists, architects, and students, and the cultivation of project-relevant links with related institutions. The MAK Center's preliminary projects—the "Architecture Again" conference held at Havana in 1994-95, whose results are to be documented in the publication "The Havana Project" and displayed in Los Angeles, and the exhibition of selected artists' editions entitled "Silent and Violent"—are exemplary of the paradigmatic change that seeks to reverse formulations and methods of procedure inasmuch as unplannable processes and encounters are to be set in motion and challenging, daring interventions substituted for a renewed use of the old and familiar.

The central question of the next few years will be how to reconcile the seclusion of the laboratory with the need to communicate and exchange information. The success of the initiative will depend on its ability to carve out a niche for itself among major international institutions, universities, and other programs, to discover and support individuals in their pioneering endeavors, and to formulate productive contacts and challenges.

Because it is sited in Los Angeles (an interface for current trends in art and architecture and a link between the cultures of Asia, South and North America, and Europe) the MAK Center for Art and Architecture is set to acquire international relevance. As an Austrian initiative aimed at exchanges of artistic activity and the imparting of major stimuli, it can, at the same time, have an important retroactive effect on Austria itself.

Finally, the MAK Center for Art and Architecture is to function not only as a central source of information about Rudolf Schindler's architecture and the current condition of his buildings, but as an assembly point and "spiritual advocate" and a kind of umbrella organization for coordinated measures.

The MAK Center Archives

The work of the Center is to be brought within the scope of "industrial communication" by means of an archive system and the gathering, recording, and storing of information in its function as a key aspect of artistic methodology. The management of data relating to artistic process and products, the preservation of what may in itself be worthless, the recording of transitional stages and processes (e.g. working models, sketches, details), and links with information networks—these are new possibilities to be explored for transcending material limitations, and non object-specific collection and dissemination. The characteristics of the global archive are the rapid actualization of data, their universal and digital availability, and the ability to access them by remote means.

The aim of the MAK Center archives is to assign central importance to questions arising from the diverse connections between artistic practice and strategies of knowledge and organization. The archive (i.e. the cataloguing, preparation, and management of data) is to assist discussion of the theoretical consideration of art and architecture in a wide context and employ it as an aid to the further development of specific themes.

Collecting data, in the sense of storing and recording current developments, should also be seen as an essential step towards the breaking of new ground. The archives are thus to be built up, not only in regard to individuals and their work but also thematically and contextually, so as to be publicly accessible in the penthouse of the Mackey Apartments by 1997.

The Mackey Apartment House (1939)

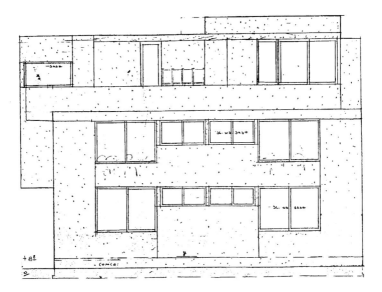

The Mackey Apartments are the home base for the MAK Center, L.A.'s artists and architects-in-residence program designed for visiting artists, architects, and students of architecture. Purchased by the Republic of Austria in 1995, the building is available for use by the MAK Center.

Located on a flat lot in a typical Los Angeles residential neighborhood, the four-unit Mackey Apartment House is one of a series of residential projects executed during the 1930s, Schindler's most productive decade. Unlike international-style architects, Schindler seldom designed identical apartment units and never repeated himself in any simple way. His apartments are as complex, individual, and innovative as the houses he planned.

The coexistence of several living units inside the Mackey House is expressed by interlocking "space forms" on the façade. Schindler manipulates form using deep walls and recessed windows to break with the typical Los Angeles flat stucco façade by means of punched openings, thereby creating a dynamic and asymmetrical composition with strong volumetric presence. The Mackey House possesses typical Schindler characteristics: compact apartment layout, exceptional incorporation of natural light, built-in furniture, variable ceiling heights, and private outdoor gardens or mini-balconies. These qualities are pronounced in the penthouse, with its entry staircase and interior balcony penetrating the two-story living-room volume, which expands to cantilever over the first floor, creating a dramatic space lit from several directions.

Although Schindler built several multi-building apartment complexes during his career, the Mackey Apartment House is notable for being a single building with multiple units and represents a good example of Schindler's later design.

Work on restoring the Mackey Apartments was started in 1995 by the Central Office of Architecture, a team of architects based in Los Angeles, and will continue for several years. During the first phase of reconstruction the building was restored to a state that corresponded as far as possible to Schindler's intentions. The architects' main aim was to recreate his room layout, complex lighting, and use of materials in respect of surfaces and color schemes. It was however not intended to restore every feature to its original condition, because that condition was neither documented nor deducible from plans, and overly expensive interventions had to be avoided. For all that, the renovation has created a surprising and refreshing general condition that testifies to Schindler's love of open spaces, airiness, and versatility.

Artists and Architects-in-Residence Program

Artists and Architects-in-Residence Program
Jury Session, MAK, Vienna, March 13, 1995, with Erika Billeter,
Gunter Damisch, Gregor Eichinger, Achille Bonito Oliva, Peter Noever

The artists and architects-in-residence program is designed for visiting artists and architects or students of architecture. Six-month residencies at the Mackey Apartments are offered to two artists and two architects, each of whom is to design and carry out a project in Los Angeles starting in October 1995. Presentations of completed works take place towards the end of each residency, and many are executed or displayed in public settings. Although not open for public tours on a regular basis, the Mackey Apartment House is available for special functions and open during project installations.

The awarding of Mackey scholarships is tied to the development of an independent project dealing with special structures between art and architecture. Taking account of space as a central category, candidates have to submit a specific proposal whose implementation and presentation forms the content of their work in Los Angeles. Four of the projects selected at the first jury session in 1995 are presented on pages 34-36. Recipients of awards are incorporated in the activities of the Schindler House and form an integral part thereof. Meetings, workshops, project discussions with other artists and students, and participation in the Center's activities are intended to bring free artistic activity within the context of institutionalized museum work and extend the boundaries of the participants' experience.

Overriding importance is attached to the siting of this program in Los Angeles. Although regarded as the USA's second artistic metropolis after New York, L.A. possesses urban and social structures that render it the most autonomous and, where the next millennium is concerned, possibly the most trendsetting example of a decentralized and unrulable urban complex. By virtue of the vast field of tension deriving from local elements—expressways, automobiles, ghettoization, social structures insusceptible of definition—the city constitutes a challenge in itself and requires a carefully calculated and complex mode of procedure. Therefore the residents' projects are to reflect and incorporate specific aspects of the city or its urban and social fabric.

One of the most important features of the Schindler initiative is its firm compliance with the principle that the initiation of processes and new projects is more relevant, within the general context of contemporary art, than their subsequent preservation by museum curators and historians. The artists and architects-in-residence program is particularly important in this respect because it presents young artists and architects with an opportunity to develop new and independent projects deriving from a study not only of Schindler's experimental work but, above all, of the specific urban situation prevailing in Los Angeles. In accordance with their stated purpose, awards function here as a precisely defined stimulus and incentive designed to activate free but focused processes and working procedures.

Schindler House

Marian Chace´s room, 1995

Clyde Chace´s room, 1995

Clyde Chace´s room, view with skylights, 1995

The Schindler House is an extraordinary object: rigorous – and, at the same time, somewhat tacky. Over the years this house has more and more come to represent (or more precisely, may indeed have triggered off) the very special spin that Los Angeles has brought to architecture. To treat tacky materials, and seemingly naive detailing, with the sternest rigour ... a contradiction in terms ... one that is almost impossible to pull off, but which is the essence of the L. A. art scene today. In that wonderful sense, the Schindler House is all what architecture should be: a self-fulfilling prophecy.

CHARLES CORREA, BOMBAY

The spirit of Schindler warms the works of all of us who were touched by his life.

FRANK O. GEHRY, LOS ANGELES

Rudolf M. Schindler was badly overlooked during his lifetime, and I must confess my part of it. I thought that Richard Neutra represented much more clearly the International Style which I was busy propagating at the Museum of Modern Art where I was the curator.

Now I believe that Schindler was a much more important figure than I had casually assumed. His place at the crossroads of art and architecture and his variety and originality of design are much greater than I gave him credit for.

He is the most important architect in California of his day and deserves highly the attention given to him at last by his hometown, Vienna.

PHILIP JOHNSON, NEW YORK

*I discovered Schindler 3 times
in my life in 3 ways
1. As a young boy, his houses were different from all the others I
saw walking through the hills in L. A.
My imagination flared.
2. As a young man learning about architecture, what it was and how
it was made.
My intellect broadened.
3. As a middle-aged man in life's transition, finding solitude and
silence in one of his houses in a space filled with light.
My heart opened up.
His works have been a gift.*

MICHAEL ROTONDI, LOS ANGELES

Rudolf Schindler was an architect inspired by ideas other architects originated and perfected. What makes him of interest today is the originality he attained within the limits of those ideas, which on a number of occasions was considerable. The sources of his originality were contradictions that arose from his efforts to integrate the diverse and disparate influences on his thought and work. The most apparent of these were European modernism, as codified in the intellectual plasticism of "De Stijl," and an American romanticism exemplified by the emotional and expressionistic buildings of Wright. Their different approaches to plasticity—the former idealized and abstract, the latter intimately tied to the specifics of site—are seen struggling without resolution in Schindler's best buildings, generating an inner tension neither would achieve alone. The lines and volumes of the Lovell Beach House, for example, could not be better suited to its site, yet at the same time the severity of their abstraction makes them seem alien, imported, otherworldly. There is a disturbing, haunting quality to such buildings, appealing to a sensibility disillusioned by dogma and formulized solutions that is more prevalent today than in Schindler's time.

There is another clash of influences worth noting in Schindlers's work, that of the planned and the anarchic city. His visionary urban schemes combine the European ideal of a controlled and coherent urban fabric and the American reality of urban sprawl spawned by uncontrolled commercialism and the automobile. While his designs did not anticipate and thus could not influence the actuality of Los Angeles' development, they projected a more dynamic and complex urbanism than that of Wright, Neutra, or any other architect of his day.

Schindler's talent for shaping form and space is evident in all his works, and this alone makes them worthy of attention and study. In the end, however, it is his failure that lifts him from his time and places him firmly in the present. His struggle with his own contradictions, never resolved, produced an architecture that instructs and inspires as never before.

LEBBEUS WOODS, NEW YORK

MAK Center Exhibitions
The Havana Project—Architecture Again (1996)

Held by MAK and the MAK Center in the winter of 1994/95 and attended by Coop Himmelb(l)au, Eric Owen Moss, Morphosis/Thom Mayne, Carme Pinós, Lebbeus Woods, and C.P.P.N. (Carl Pruscha, Peter Noever), this conference —or, rather, working meeting—concentrated on the need to redefine the role of architecture and to reveal the possibilities and social applications of constructed space, this being the primary and central purpose of architecture, rather than relying on the unlimited and seductive possibilities of new technologies and material abundance.

In the course of the conference, all the participating architects developed concrete projects, planned interventions in Havana's urban structure whose common feature is an almost symbiotic fusion with the city and its living fabric. All these projects are based on the existing structure and every design makes use of existing architectural substance: no destruction, no unbounded self-expression, but a transformation of what exists, a respectful reforming of the substance already there. The first presentation of these unique architectural projects constitutes, at the same time, the inaugural exhibition of the MAK Center for Art and Architecture in April 1996.

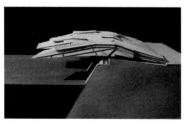

Lebbeus Woods: Model of the Malécon Terrace, Project for Havana, 1995

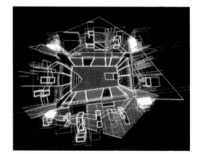

Eric Moss: Computer drawing of the Plaza Nueva Vieja, Project for Havana, 1995

Presentation of the city model of Havana Architecture Again, International Conference on Art and Architecture Havana/Cuba,` Dec. 30, 1994–Jan. 5, 1995

Silent & Violent—Selected Artists' Editions (1996)

The exhibition entitled "Silent and Violent—Selected Artists' Editions" is intended to address the diversity and openness of contemporary art, thereby endorsing the antidogmatism of current creative activities that are more concerned with abolishing restrictive definitions of art than lamenting the loss of an aura. Over sixty of the most internationally significant and controversial artists are represented by editions that employ a wide diversity of media ranging from photography and various printing processes, to new media such as video and computer graphics, even including to the alienation of everyday materials in multiples.

That sixty artists of the most diverse orientation and working methods should have taken part in this project, which was initiated by *Parkett*, the Swiss art magazine, testifies to a common quest for innovative possibilities devoid of strict definition. It also shows how futile and reversible demarcations and prohibitions governing the traditional notion of art are, vis-à-vis the creative experiments with the reproductive processes of our age.

1

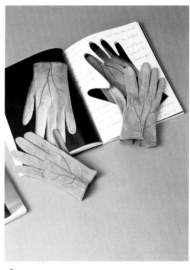

2

3

1. Robert Gober, Untitled, *1991. Lithograph on newsprint with hand-torn edges, 75/XXV unique pieces*

2. Meret Oppenheim, Glove, *1985. Goat suede with silk-screen, hand-stitched, Edition 150/XII*

3. Christian Boltanski, El Caso, 1989. Booklet with 17 photographs, Edition 80/XX

Mackey Apartment Building

View of Pearl Mackey Apartment House from Cochran Avenue, 1995

*Interior View of Mackey
Apartments, 1995*

*Interior View of Mackey
Apartments,1995*

Interior View of Mackey Apartments, 1995

The Garage Project

The first of a series of independent artists' projects to be carried out at the Mackey House, with or without the participation of artists and architects-in-residence, are presented at the initial exhibition entitled "The Garage Project". The four installations by Peter Kogler (Vienna), Liz Larner (Los Angeles); Paul McCarthy (Los Angeles), and Heimo Zobernig (Vienna) had, as their point of departure, the Mackey House's existing garage spaces. Four simple units constructed of redwood planks formed the basis of four autonomous artistic interventions that were developed independently of each other but took account of the spatial situation common to them all and to Rudolf Schindler's underlying architectural visions.

PAUL McCARTHY
DIAGNOSIS AND DISSECTION: the garage as a creepy mini-theater, a viewing room for film and video. Visual fragments—referring to the physical structure of the Mackey House, to Schindler's life, friends and work, and to his back-to-nature/physical fitness ethic—address issues of control and correction, dress and undress. (Work in progress)

LIZ LARNER
THE CENTURY PLANT (Agave Americana): the enigmatic Century Plant dominant in L.A.'s landscape of the 30s grows for 10 years before erupting into bloom for one great season, after which it dies, leaving an exoskeleton that preserves the blossoming form. Placing this trace of L.A.'s lost landscape in the midst of the human detritus of the abandoned garage makes the symbolic vision of a park or garden as part of today's living space. (Work in progress)

PETER KOGLER
SCHINDLER DISCOTHEQUE: The surface area of one of the garages at Mackey House can be doubled by means of a pink-colored, pull-out curtain construction and transformed into a disco. Pink was not Schindler's favorite color but that of his wife, Pauline.

HEIMO ZOBERNIG
UNTITLED: A garage is a garage, even when it's a Schindler garage: practical, aesthetic, metaphorical for the automobile; as a workroom, store, bar, or gallery. When the door is opened next to the Schindler Discotheque, tables and chairs—made of fittings in the garage, such as shelves, etc.—can be taken out, the telescopic bar extended into the open air and opened for business (the Schindler Bar with Schindler Drinks).

Illustrations: Peter Kogler: Sample of material for Schindler curtain, 1995
Liz Larner: Photo of a Century Plant; Paul McCarthy: Grand Pop, *1977*
Heimo Zobernig: Galerie Trabant, *1994*

The Garage Project, Mackey House, Los Angeles 1996

33

Artists and Architects-in-Residence Program, Mackey House Projects

Swetlana Heger and Plamen Dejanov
L.A.,CA City Apartment, 500 sq. meters + terrace. US $20,000 (1995/96)

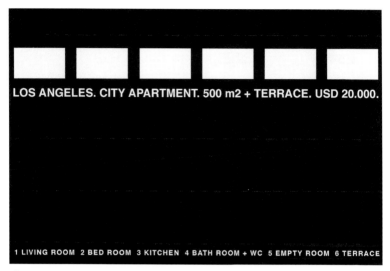

Computer generated drawing, 1994

A virtual "apartment" consisting of six separate "rooms" is to be installed in various locations in L.A.. The urban rooms are defined by individual sculptural elements, distributed over an area of several hundred square meters and incorporating available infrastructure and public furnishings. The rooms are temporarily inhabitable and aim to redefine our concept of living environments: the exterior spaces take over the function of the interior spaces—the borders between private/public and inside/outside dissolve. The installation is conceived not only to fill the unused gaps of the city functionally but also to occupy them conceptually. Advertisements (see project title) constitute part of the artists' public presentation of the project and can be found in (American) daily newspapers and magazines.

Andrea Lenardin—ConsumptionMuseum (1996)

ConsumptionMuseum is a collection of materials, an inventory of ideas exploring the borderlines between architecture, media reality, virtual identity, consumption, and art. The overwhelming flood of visual images—mixing information and representation (appearance and reality) in instant replay—voids the boundaries between previously separated levels of experience. Fleetingness no longer allows time and space to determine reality.

The surreal "user friendly" surfaces, where the concept and its presentation are perceived as equal, ignore the conflict between thesis and anti-thesis.

The goal of the *ConsumptionMuseum* is to disturb the flood of visual images, to take the singular out of the stereotypical flood, thereby giving it autonomous presence.

Studies for ConsumptionMuseum – *Project photos, Vienna, June 26, 1994*

Christoph Kasperkovitz
Apparence of deficiency (1996)

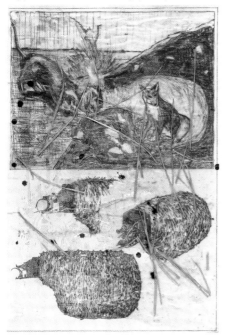

Apparence of deficiency consists of two human-sized objects ("dwellings") created out of woven material, straw, feathers, clay, tar, wax, buried into the ground, representing in form an animals' den. Placed at their openings, facing inside, two video monitors project specific sound and visual material into the space. From the outside, through the unpatched cracks of the "dwelling," the viewer will only perceive the blue reflections, in varying intensity.

Blueprint no. 1, acrylic, straw, stain, 1995

Gilbert Bretterbauer
Mysterious heritage in the surroundings of L.A. (1996)

Collage, 1995

The utopian fabric house to be realized in an isolated canyon in the surround-ings of L.A. incorporates elementary aspects of traditional architectural space and nomadic forms of housing, but dissolves at the same time the tectonics and the functionality of built structure. Colored fabric surfaces, variable shapes, transparency, and mobility describe the fluid and conceptual bound-aries of a mysterious place of intimacy, a primary, immaterial dwelling. Without solid walls, without claim to a specific site and without permenance, the fabric house absorbs its exterior—by reversing the parameters of inside/outside—and becomes an in-between space for emotional/aesthetic experience.

His House, Her House, Their House

Robert L. Sweeney

When Pauline Schindler established a non-profit organization to preserve the Kings Road house in 1976, she had lived there on and off for fifty-four years, twenty-three years longer than Schindler himself. She had created her own active life at the house, so drastically altering the appearance of the building in the process that it had become more a statement of her occupancy than his. Still, the assumption at the time was that she was saving an icon of modern architecture while ensuring the reputation of her former husband, with whom she had had an unorthodox relationship at best but whose gift as an architect she readily acknowledged.

Today Mrs. Schindler's motivation seems more complex and more personal. Certainly she never lost sight of the significance of the building or its function as an architectural laboratory. Schindler worked here until his death, establishing a legacy of progressive design in Southern California as we know it today and far exceeding the footprint left by his mentor Frank Lloyd Wright, who preceded him. Still, it was perhaps as a gathering spot for cultural and political ferment that the house had greatest meaning for Mrs. Schindler. Though clearly Schindler gave architectural form to the house and was sympathetic with the lifestyle it embodied, it now seems clear that much of the social theory was determined by his wife. In 1916—three years before she met Schindler—she wrote to her mother, describing the sort of democratic meeting place she hoped to live in; her ideal was realized at Kings Road. Finally, for RMS and Pauline it was home; both maintained a tenacious grip.

The House as Laboratory

Schindler lived and worked at Kings Road until his death in 1953. Eclipsed during his lifetime by Wright and Richard Neutra, his evolution as a designer is increasingly viewed as one of the great episodes in the history of twentieth-century architecture. Generally he worked alone; the one notable exception was a partnership in the twenties with Richard Neutra. The idea of collaboration was appealing; in late 1925 Schindler wrote that it would enable them "...to undertake larger industrial buildings...."[1] The association formed in 1926 was called "The Architectural Group for Industry and Commerce."

At the time, Schindler was working on three houses for Philip Lovell: a beach house, a mountain cottage, and a ranch house. A large city house was to follow in 1927. Today we recognize the beach house as Schindler's supreme achievement. A project of far greater potential, however, was a competition entry for the League of Nations building in Geneva. Schindler and Neutra worked on the design between August 1926 and January 1927. They produced an asymmetrical constructivist composition in which each of the two major components—secretariat and assembly hall—is clearly articulated in plan and elevation; the most dramatic feature is the secretariat with its stepped floors cantilevering over a lake. Theirs was one of 377 entries submitted;

they learned in May that they had not received any of the prizes that were awarded.

The thirties were lean for Schindler; like most architects, he built little. He told Frank Lloyd Wright in December 1930 that he was "...still struggling along, scheming, designing, building...mostly scheming." Of course, the current economic doldrums precluded any real chance of significant work, but also Schindler had adopted a passive attitude toward obtaining his architect's license. He first applied in 1921 and was rejected; he put the matter aside until 1929, when he asked for Wright's assistance. Wright, noting that he had recommended Schindler as a competent architect several years earlier, responded this time with "Samples...to choose from." Some of the passages were helpful, others were less than likely to further the cause:

> I appreciate Rudolf. He is an incorrigible Bohemian and refuses to allow the Los Angeles barber to apply the razor to the scruff of his neck. He also has peculiarly simple and effective ideas regarding his own personal conduct.

And:

> It's a damn'd shame that you fellows have refused Schindler a license all these years.
> He is worth any ten of you and he would be justified were he sitting where you sit ... in refusing you a license to practice anything but drafting in some old-fashioned architect's office.[2]

Schindler responded: *If this will not get me into any architectural heaven, Saint Peter must have lost his keys. I only protest against your mental picture of the scruff of my neck, it's not as hairy as a real 'artiste' would like it.* [3]

For Schindler architectural heaven was a long time coming. Unlike Wright and Neutra, he never mastered the art of self-promotion; perhaps most stinging was his repudiation by the organizers of the Modern Architecture exhibition at the Museum of Modern Art in New York in 1932. Henry-Russell Hitchcock and Philip Johnson commented in the catalogue that "R. M. Schindler in California, although trained in Europe, belongs rather with the group of Wright's followers."[4]

Philip Johnson especially was unimpressed. He paid his first and only visit to Kings Road in 1931; he reflected some sixty years later:

> I went to Los Angeles in 1931, primarily to see Richard Neutra, before the "Modern Architecture" exhibition. Neutra was really evil, badmouthed everybody, especially Schindler. I went to see Schindler at his house. I didn't like the house, it looked cheap and the housekeeping wasn't good. Based on these impressions and what Neutra had said, I didn't go to see anything else by Schindler.

He continued:

> I've still never seen his work. But I realize now my mistake. This man was an artist.[5]

One has to wonder if Johnson's revisionist attitude today would extend to the Kings Road house. He didn't say so.

Only towards the end of the thirties did Schindler's career revive. In spite of this relative inactivity, his long-time friend Ellen Janson was able to discuss a wide range of accomplishments in an essay written in 1939. She observed the contrast between the Kings Road house and other early modern work that "...was rigidly adhering to the classical syntax of base and shaft and crown..." She continued that "like all innovators..," Schindler often worked under difficult circumstances, but he still "...never compromised." "Slowly and surely he has developed his technique, based on what he calls his form vocabulary." [6]

Schindler followed up with his own assessment in 1949, identifying thirty of his works that seemed "...to have special architectural interest and historical meaning in the development of contemporary architecture." He referred specifically to experiments with new materials and techniques and concluded that "You will find that most of the houses I include illustrate early uses of some of the techniques so much in favor today...." He paid special homage to the Kings Road house, citing it as a summary of his principles. Notably slighting Wright's work in Southern California, Schindler instead suggested that he had continued the precedent set by Irving Gill, " ...the only local architect who had made any consistent effort to break with tradition and the fashionable 'Spanish Style'...."[7]

Significantly, all of the buildings Schindler listed were either houses or small commercial buildings. The "...larger industrial buildings..." he had envisioned in 1925 did not materialize. This, coupled with his inability to attract a more affluent clientele, is perhaps the tragedy of Schindler, explaining his position in the wings and not on center stage where he surely belonged. In retrospect, his willingness to work with small budgets and cheap materials served him poorly; much of his work has not aged gracefully. We can only speculate on this man's ability to carry out a truly grand design.

The House as Meeting-Place

One of my dreams, Mother, is to have, some day, a little joy of a bungalow, on the edge of woods and mountains and near a crowded city, which shall be open just as some people´s hearts are open, to friends of all classes and types. I should like it to be as democratic a meeting-place as Hull-House, where millionaires and laborers, professors and illiterates, the splendid and the ignoble meet constantly together.
Sophie Pauline Gibling to her mother, May 1916[8]

With this newly discovered statement we gain an entirely new perspective on the formative process of the Kings Road house. Pauline Schindler's concept of egalitarianism, the analogy with Hull House where she was then working, and the concept of a communal lifestyle imparted a theoretical framework to the house just as surely as Schindler provided three-dimensional resolution.

Perhaps it was no accident that she married an architect.

In the twenties and early thirties, the gatherings at Kings Road seem to have been primarily artistic in focus. Two days after Richard and Dione Neutra moved in, the Schindlers organized a supper party for them. Maynard Dixon, by then well established as a Southwest artist, attended. Another dinner in the summer of 1925 honored Mrs. Archipenko, wife of the artist. Later that year Maurice Brown, an English playwright and actor who had started the Chicago Little Theater in 1912, lectured at Kings Road; a party followed. Pauline Schindler described it to her mother: "...(it is) going to be huge. We have never had more than a hundred guests before. But this will be overflowing." After the party, she remembered "...all the fires burning brightly and the evening warm enough for the house to be wide open."[9]

Pauline Schindler's room with original furniture by R.M. Schindler, 1920s

Some of the entertainment at Kings Road was more avant-garde. John Bovingdon, who lived in the house between 1926 and 1931, first in the guest apartment, then in the larger Chace apartment, and his wife Jeanya are remembered for their "progressive dances" in the garden. Dione Neutra described one performance in 1926:

It was a lovely sight. Against the sky, forming the background, different sounding gongs in various sizes hung from twelve poles. The dancer, clad only in a loin cloth made out of batik, sounded these gongs in ten-minute intervals, gracefully and in slow motion, moving between them. Then he started to dance, portraying primitive man before he was walking upright or could use his hands; first writhing on the ground, then in an ecstasy of joy, discovering that he could walk erect. All this without music. It was very gripping in the open landscape.[10]

Sadakichi Hartmann, a self-described "...mad, bad, sad and slightly red poet," was another member of Schindler's inner circle. He lived a penurious existence, regularly asked Schindler for a dollar or two, and was described by Edward Weston in 1928 as "...a sad old ruin...who was paying for a dissipated, malicious life...." Still he obviously amused Schindler, who allowed him to use the house for "readings" to which the public was invited. At "A Poe Evening" in January 1928, Hartmann announced that he would read "A Tell-Tale Heart" and other short stories, "provided he does not change his mind." The announcement continued that "Mr. Hartmann will endeavor to look like Edgar Allen Poe." On another evening the topic was modern art; the public was advised that "This will be the most amusing Art Talk of the season; miss it if you can."[11]

Later there was a decided shift from avant-garde cultural events to left-

Announcement flyer for Sadakichi Hartmann´s lecture at the Schindler House

wing political activism at Kings Road. This was the domain of Pauline Schindler; the interest in bringing together "all classes and types" expressed in 1916 in fact became rather specifically focused on the likes of Robert Oppenheimer and Haakon Chevalier. In the fifties Mrs. Schindler sponsored a series of "Discussions in a Garden," which she publicized with postcards of her own design. Martin Hall spoke on the Korean conflict in 1950; Dr. Alexander Kaun addressed "Morale in the Soviet Union" in 1952. Also in 1952 West Hollywood Democrats for Wallace met at the house; guests were promised "songs of political action and the common man." Pauline Schindler's papers are intact; hopefully the history of her later years at Kings Road is forthcoming.

The House as Home

The undertaking began as an experiment in communal living; two couples would live under the same roof and share one kitchen. The other couple were Clyde and Marian Chace; before their marriages, Sophie Pauline Gibling and Marian DaCamara had attended Smith College, class of 1915. Both women left Smith with active interests in progressive social and political causes, and within five years both had married.

The Schindlers arrived in Los Angeles from the Midwest in December 1920, the Chaces in the summer of 1921. By November plans for the joint venture had been worked out, and in January 1922 a building site was acquired. The property on Kings Road was on the outskirts of Hollywood. Located in the flatlands, it offered views of the Santa Monica Mountains and an unobstructed horizon to the west; early photographs confirm that it was a far less surprising choice then than it seems now. It was purchased from Walter Luther Dodge, whose own grand house to the north, designed in 1916 by Irving Gill, suggested that Kings Road would indeed become an address of substance. The details of the arrangement were formalized in an agreement signed by both couples on February 11, 1922. The Schindlers and Chaces were to "...join in a cooperative enterprise for owning land and for building thereon a home...." Upon completion of the house, the parties were to occupy and live in separate portions of it; other portions were to be used jointly. A separate guest apartment was to be used by either party or their guests or friends. It was agreed that "...the architectural services shall be furnished by R.M. Schindler," and that "...Clyde Chace will furnish his services as contractor and have control over [sic] the erection of the building in accordance with the plans and specifications."[12]

The house was constructed between February and June 1922; there was an intriguing relationship with Irving Gill, who presumably came to help with the "slab-tilt" construction. A completion notice was filed June 6.[13]

Clyde and Marian Chace were the first occupants; they moved into the guest apartment in May before their own space was finished. They remained at Kings Road just over two years; during that period Clyde also built Schindler's Popenoe house in Coachella and the Pueblo Ribera Court in La Jolla. Late in life he recalled that because of this building activity, he and his wife were often away, but that the relationship with the Schindlers was amicable. He did mention that the Schindlers and his wife liked to go to bed much later than he.[14]

Richard and Dione Neutra left a much more complete—and entertaining—record of life at Kings Road. They lived there between March 1925 and December 1930, first in the guest apartment, then in the Chace apartment. Something of the tenor of their stay comes from contemporary correspondence and from more recent conversations with Mrs. Neutra and her sister, Regula Fybel, who also lived at the house.[15] The portrait is one of idealism tempered by lack of money and physical discomfort and of extreme differences in the temperaments of the players.

The house itself was both spiritually rewarding and distressing to deal with. Neutra described the romance of sleeping in the open in March 1927:

I glance from my sleeping porch into the spring greenery. It has rained yesterday and this night. The leaves of our trumpet vine glisten with rain drops. The huge bamboo stalks—together with a contingent of birds, who, with their twittering, apply the colorful background music to Dione's songs —sway gently in the breeze. Now my gaze focuses on the feathery foliage of a young pepper tree that peeps over the roof and a reddish climbing rose whips gently near Dion's (the Neutra's son) chimney.

Earlier Neutra addressed a reality of the house that continues to exist today.

Marion Chace's room, 1920s

"The roof leaks quite badly in two places. Rain falls through the fireplace which thus becomes a waterplace."[16]

For her part, Dione Neutra found that the "...strange house ...has its own beauty...," but "an aggravation is that the apartment is so impractical." She elaborated in a letter to her mother:

I wrote you a letter yesterday which I am now absolutely unable to find because I have no desk, unfortunately. It can hardly be expected in a Schindler house. His residences are not designed for children, as he does not think about them, and not for people who write, because he hardly ever writes himself. Richard has a kind of workroom which is, however, filled with his own stuff, thus there is no vacant shelf for me....[17]

The Schindlers and the Neutras were all strong personalities. Pauline Schindler and Dione Neutra learned early on that they could not share the communal kitchen. Schindler responded with a design for a small new kitchen in the Neutra apartment; it was in place by late 1926. Dione Neutra described it as consisting "...of two boards covered with oilcloth, supported by two wood blocks. It is primitive but suffices."[18] Vestiges—a drain pipe and discolorations in the concrete walls and floor—can be seen today. Most serious was the bitter split between Schindler and Neutra in 1930.

In March 1931 Galka Scheyer succeeded the Bovingdons as tenant of the Chace apartment, unhappily sharing the space with them for a short time. She had a remarkable collection of paintings and drawings by The Blue Four—the artists Feininger, Jawlensky, Kandinsky, and Klee—now owned by the Norton Simon Museum in Pasadena.

Galka Scheyer in Marian Chace's room, 1931/32

She was not a stranger: she had lived briefly in the guest apartment in the summer of 1927. In November 1930 she contacted Schindler again, explaining that she was about to return to Los Angeles from Bali and that she needed a big room with light and wall space in which to live. She had purchased "...a marvelous collection of Bali things —mostly paintings," which she wanted to display. By then she had as well a large collection of works by avant-garde artists including not only The Blue Four but Archipenko, Dix, Kokoschka, Lissitzky, Marc, Moholy-Nagy, Nolde, and Schlemmer. She wrote to Kandinsky in August 1931 that she was cataloging the collection and was "...already up to no. 326."[19]

Kandinsky, having heard descriptions of the Kings Road house, responded enthusiastically to Scheyer: "The Weisshaus couple, who were here recently, talked to us in detail about your house; location, sliding walls, etc. It really must be very beautiful, and we are happy that you live in such a grandiose manner. 'Galka understands it!'...."[20]

In fact, as Dione Neutra had earlier, Galka Scheyer found that living in the Kings Road house required adjustment. She wrote to Schindler in April 1931 that she had rented the house for $60 a month expecting "...liveable conditions; namely, with circulation which does not necessitate climbing on the roof to open or close a window...," and that "...a window opening to the front is a normal human condition which any human being would request in a normal house. That people like the Bovingtons [*sic*], who are Bohemians, lived like they lived is an exception and of no advantage either to you or your house. I am not a Bohemian." Still, she was able to tell Jawlensky in August 1932 that "The local summer is beautiful, not too hot. I run around in the nude all day long and feel very much at ease." [21]

Galka Scheyer's statement was revealing; during the thirties, the Kings Road house assumed a decidedly Bohemian atmosphere. No doubt the breakdown in the lifestyle as it was originally envisioned was largely responsible: Pauline Schindler left her husband abruptly in 1927, taking their son Mark and moving to Carmel. After the departure of the Neutras, the house was physically divided to turn the Chace apartment into a completely separate rental unit. Numerous tenants passed through; the level of discipline imparted by Pauline and the Neutras was not sustained by the less interested parties who followed.

Still, Mrs. Schindler weaved in and out of the scenario at Kings Road between 1927 and 1938, when she returned permanently. She controlled the Chace apartment; in February 1932 she acidly informed Galka Scheyer that "...r.m.s. has at no time been authorized by me to enter into any contract, written or otherwise, concerning the disposition of our joint property," and " that i should soon be needing the apartment you are at present occupying. it will not be possible for you to choose with which of the owners of this property you will deal in these matters." [22]

Pauline's need for the apartment at the time is unclear, although she and Mark did return to live at the house several times between 1927 and 1938. She may have had in mind renting it to her friend John Cage, though Cage himself remembered hearing of the vacancy through an acquaintance. He and his companion, Don Sample, lived in the house for less than a year; Cage found that it was "clearly a modern house, but...an extraordinary house, particularly in its details.... All the details of nature are present." Referring to the extraordinary openness of the plan, he recalled liking "being in one place and seeing another." Cage also recalled a romantic liaison with Pauline; she in turn reported to her mother in 1934 that he had visited her in Ojai for eight or nine days and had written a sonata which he dedicated to her. [23]

Mary MacLaren was another memorable tenant; she was a silent-screen actress who rented the guest apartment between 1930 and 1935. Schindler met her at the Braxton Art Gallery where she had a part-time job, and ultimately invited her to move into Kings Road; late in life she recalled loving him very much. She left after a fire at the house in October 1935, caused by an overheated hot water tank. By then, however, the relationship seems to have run its course: responding to a request for cash for clothing that was destroyed, Schindler reminded her that she "...left the apartment not clean as far as the dirt goes, but absolutely cleaned out as far as the equipment goes." He continued that "...since your sister replaced a large part of your second hand clothes I do not see how you are much worse off now as before the fire...." [24]

Surely the most entertainingly flamboyant occupant was Samson De Brier, a self-styled "gentleman of leisure." He was there during World War II; like so

Virginia Blakeley, Peggy Maurey,   *Samson De Brier*
Samson De Brier in the guest apart-
ment, ca.1944

many of the tenants, he came to the house less out of sympathy for its principles than because there was a vacancy. Interviewed in 1983, he recalled a
visit from his brother, a U.S. Army general, who refused to go inside the house
when he saw mail from "Russian organizations" addressed to Mrs. Schindler
in the shared mail box. De Brier also claimed to have starred in a mildly off-
color movie shot in the guest apartment by his friend, the filmmaker Kenneth
Anger. Anger subsequently denied the existence of this film.[25]

Pauline Schindler essentially lived away from Kings Road for eleven
years. After leaving Carmel, she returned to Los Angeles, moving into Frank
Lloyd Wright's Storer House, then owned by a bank. Later, she drifted
between Los Angeles and Ojai, where Mark was in school. Her return to Kings
Road coincided with divorce proceedings initiated by her husband. In a living
arrangement that seems amusing today, she occupied the Chace apartment;
Schindler remained in his original space. She had custody of the kitchen.
From this point on, their lives appear to have been almost entirely separate.
Although Mrs. Schindler understood the house intellectually, she could not live
in it as designed; she worked on it constantly until her death, literally covering
every surface. Most galling to Schindler was her paint; he addressed the issue
in 1949:

Madam:

I hear you want me to select a color for the painting of Kings Road.
You understand that Kings Road was built as a protest against the
American habit of covering their life and their buildings with coats of finish
material to fool the onlooker about the common base. Kings Road was
conceived as a combination of honest materials, concrete — redwood —
glass, which were to be left to show the inner structure, and their natural
color.

The house is the first example of the type of modern dwelling which is not repeated endlessly, and as such has some historical interest.

I realize that you have fought from the beginning against the character and the exxence [*sic*] of the house, and the painting of the outside aged redwood in a contrasting color would be a final stab in the back.

If you paint your part of the house, and I wish you would restrict yourself to that, my struggle for expressions and the resistance of the unsensitive [*sic*] would receive another monument.

Sincerely, [26]

Post Script

Pauline Schindler died in 1977. She left in place an organization that would succeed her as keeper of the Kings Road house; the property was acquired from her estate in 1980 with funding from the California Office of Historic Preservation. Money for restoration has come from the State of California and the City of West Hollywood; much progress has been made, much remains to be done. The work accomplished so far in relation to the money spent caused Paul Goldberger to comment that the house is probably the biggest bargain in the history of preservation. There to write a Sunday column for the *New York Times* about the restoration, he continued that he had always known it was a great house, but that now he could *see* it.

Work continues. On the evening of August 17, 1994, a celebration was held at Kings Road on the occasion of the signing of a cooperation agreement between Friends of the Schindler House and the MAK-Austrian Museum of Applied Arts, Vienna. At the heart of the agreement is the creation of a center for art and architecture at the house, a concept entirely in keeping with the founding goals of FOSH. A corollary exchange program reinforces the link between Vienna and Los Angeles. This agreement will carry the house — and Schindler — into the twenty-first century.

Notes

1 R.M. Schindler to Mr. and Mrs. Gibling, Christmas 1925, Pauline Schindler
   Collection, currently in the possession of Lionel and Maureen Vidler
   March. The Marches are kindly thanked for their cooperation with this
   article.
2 Schindler to Frank Lloyd Wright, December 16, 1930. Schindler to Wright,
   April 11, 1929. Wright to Architectural Review Board, August 7, 1929.
   Wright to Architectural Review Board, August 7, 1929.
   Frank Lloyd Wright Foundation, Scottsdale, Arizona.
3 Schindler to Wright, August 16, 1929. Frank Lloyd Wright Foundation.
4 Philip Johnson and Henry-Russell Hitchcock, Jr., "The Extent of Modern
   Architecture," *Modern Architecture, International Exhibition*
   (New York, Museum of Modern Art, 1932), p. 22.
5 Philip Johnson to author, personal communication, New York,
   June 23, 1988.
6 EJ (Ellen Janson), "Biographical Notes on R.M. Schindler Architect,"
   R.M. Schindler Architect, privately published, 1949, pp. 2, 3.
7 R.M. Schindler to The School of Architecture, University of Southern
   California, Los Angeles, California, October 10, 1949.
   Reproduced in *R.M. Schindler Architect,* pp. 1, 2.
8 Sophie Pauline Gibling to her mother, May 1916.
   Pauline Schindler Collection, currently in the possession of
   Lionel and Maureen Vidler March.
9 Gibling to parents, March 10, 1925. Schindler to Gibling, summer 1925.
   Gibling to parents, October 1, 1925. Gibling to parents, October 1925.
   Gibling to parents, no date. Pauline Schindler Collection, currently in the
   possession of Lionel and Maureen Vidler March.
10 On February 6, 1926, Pauline wrote to her parents that Bovingdon had
   recently arrived from Java. Letter currently in the possession of Lionel and
   Maureen Vidler March. The description of Bovingdon's performance is in
   Dione to Muetterli, October 1926; quoted in *Richard Neutra Promise and
   Fulfillment, 1919-1932. Selections from the Letters and Diaries of Richard
   and Dione Neutra.(* Compiled and translated by Dione Neutra. Carbondale
   and Edwardsville: Southern Illinois University Press, 1986,) p. 157.
11 Hartmann. *The Daybooks of Edward Weston.* I. Mexico. II. California.
   Edited by Nancy Newhall. Forward by Beaumont Newhall.(New York:
   Aperture, 1990), p.61. The *Daybooks* contain other references to
   Schindler and his circle, including a humorous account of Galka Scheyer
   and Weston switching clothes at a party.
12 Agreement, February 11, 1922, R.M. Schindler Collection, Architectural
   Drawing Collection, University of California, Santa Barbara.
13 Irving Gill's specific role, if any, in the construction of the Kings Road
   house is unclear. He was invited there for a picnic in one undated and
   unsigned letter; another letter, undated but circa May 1922, contains a
   reference to his "next visit." Notice of Completion, June 6, 1922.

R.M. Schindler Collection, Architectural Drawing Collection, University of California, Santa Barbara.

14 Kimmie (Marian Chace) to Gibling, no date. R.M. Schindler Collection, Architectural Drawing Collection, University of California, Santa Barbara. Kathryn Smith and Robert L. Sweeney, interview with Clyde Chace, July 28, 1987.

15 Nancy J. Sanquist and I interviewed Dione Neutra on April 8, 1982. We met with Regula Fybel on February 21, 1983. I had numerous informal conversations with both women in subsequent years.

16 Neutra to Muetterli, March 1927. Neutra to Vreneli and Ruben, December 1926. Quoted in *Richard Neutra Promise and Fulfillment 1919–1932*, pp. 158, 164.

17 Dione Neutra to Frances Toplitz, February 1925; Dione to Vreneli, June 1926; Dione to Muetterli, April 1926; quoted in *Richard Neutra Promise and Fulfillment 1919–1932*, pp. 136, 149, 154.

18 Dione Neutra to Muetterli, October 1926; quoted in *Richard Neutra Promise and Fulfillment 1919–1932*, p. 158.

19 Galka Scheyer to Schindler, November 11, 1930. R.M. Schindler Collection, Architectural Drawing Collection, University of California, Santa Barbara. Scheyer to Kandinsky, August 1931, The Blue Four Galka Scheyer Collection, Norton Simon Museum, Pasadena. Nancy J. Sanquist helped me sort through this material on December 20, 1982.

20 Kandinsky to Scheyer, no date, The Blue Four Galka Scheyer Collection, Norton Simon Museum, Pasadena.

21 Scheyer to Schindler, April 12, 1931, R.M. Schindler Collection, Architectural Drawing Collection, University of California, Santa Barbara. Scheyer to Jawlensky, August 1932, The Blue Four Galka Scheyer Collection, Norton Simon Museum, Pasadena.

22 Pauline Schindler to Galka Scheyer, February 14, 1932, R.M. Schindler Collection, Architectural Drawing Collection, University of California, Santa Barbara.

23 Mark Schindler to author, personal communication, September 6, 1995. Thomas S. Hines, "Then Not Yet 'Cage': The Los Angeles Years, 1912–1938," *John Cage—Composed in America.* Edited by Marjorie Perloff and Charles Junkerman, (Chicago and London: The University of Chicago Press, 1994), pp. 81–85. Pauline Schindler to her mother, January 25, 1934, courtesy of Friends of the Schindler House.

24 Mary MacLaren to Robert L. Sweeney, personal communication, January 30, 1983. Schindler to MacLaren, December 31, 1935, R.M. Schindler Collection, Architectural Drawing Collection, University of California, Santa Barbara.

25 I interviewed Samson De Brier on February 18, 1983, and spoke to Kenneth Anger on the telephone a short time after.

26 Schindler to Pauline Schindler, April 8, 1949. R.M. Schindler Collection, Architectural Drawing Collection, University of California, Santa Barbara.

The Schindlers en route to Los Angeles

We thought we were living in a novel!

Johannes Gachnang

They called him Jeremy and he came from Switzerland. He has never been to California. The farthest west he ever stopped is Marfa, Texas. But he knows about the West Coast from the marvellous writings of Blaise Cendrars *(L'Or)*, Dashiel Hammett *(The Thin Man)*, and Charles Olson *(Call Me Ishmael)*. The environs of Los Angeles are no blank page to him either because of the tales told by the two artists, William N. Copley and James Lee Byars.

All of this never took him to Kings Road in Hollywood, but it did bring him closer. Details he learned from his girlfriend, Rebecca, who had set out many years ago with the firm intention of starting a new life in San Francisco. After a long and arduous journey from Warsaw via Naples and Vienna, she ended up in Brussels instead. He realized that she knew a great many people whom she loved, and for just that reason he loved Rebecca.

He learned more from a furniture designer and art collector, for whom Gerrit Rietveld had built a home years ago in the wooded heartland of southern Holland. It was he who had sent a brochure to Antwerp five summers previously, titled *R.M. Schindler House: 1921-22* and with a dedication to Jeremy in it. In the accompanying letter, he found an affinity between the house in Kings Road and not only Rietveld's Pavilion for the Sonsbeek Exhibition (1954) but also his furniture designs. As this friend of the Dutch architect has it, Rietveld designed a piece of furniture every two years in order to test the viability of his architecture. After each such interlude (Exercice de style), the art collector tells us, Rietveld always produced his best architectural designs.

The small, thin pamphlet with its wonderful and wondrous illustrations instantly appealed to Jeremy. He would have loved to ride to California on horseback in order to build a house there for a beautiful woman. He would stroll about the construction site every day with a sketchbook and tools, so that living there upon completion, they would create a shared spiritual and sensual identity. He leafed through the booklet for a very long time trying to decipher the mystery he sensed was there. He was less interested in the architecture than in the compelling, individual demands embodied in the house pictured there and generating a

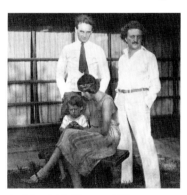

Left to right: Dion and Dione Neutra, Richard Neutra, and R.M. Schindler, in the court of the Schindler House, 1928

contagious atmosphere that infects the viewer. Being a modern man, Jeremy xeroxed the booklet and mailed the copied pages to his girlfriend Rebecca exiled in Brussels, hoping that she would soon send him additional news on the subject and on California. Hearing nothing from her for a long time, he finally went back to the pictures on his own; they told him tales of secret but also fulfilled dreams and less frequently of emotional injuries. He looked so hard that he forgot and lost the other story. Until one day—like Kokoschka's *Bride of the Winds*—Rebecca appeared in the doorway, angry and imperious, wanting to know what all this was supposed to be about: he just wanted to travel with her and not live with her, didn't he? The grand entrance of this enchanting woman initially rendered him speechless, but he thought she would probably soon reveal all to him: perhaps in a manner as if it were her wont to live grandly in the face of death.

The pent-up tensions gradually subsided; they sat down at the table in the garden to take a new look—this time together—and talk about the pictures of the Californian dream. Out of the blue, Rebecca began talking about her distant home in Poland and her memories of glorious days spent in Zakopane with her parents, who frequented the same circles as the writer and artist Stanislaw Ignacy Witkiewcz. Once again she spoke about finally traveling on to California.

Her words sounded urgent, almost beseeching. A decision was pending, a challenge menacingly suspended in space. She wanted to go West, but he was drawn to the East—two irreconcilable opposites. Pouring over houses and floor plans, she was bravely making plans for her future on the West Coast of America. Once she had reached the destination of her desires, the Far East with its rich and varied cultures would be closer as well—from the other, the western side.

But Jeremy could not shake his apprehension about these vistas. Weren't the pictures and messages connected with this house all illusory? Were they prisoners of an age whose eloquence belongs to other places and other sites, now hardly cognizant of its former intentions and qualities? Is it even possible to preserve the spirit of pictures passed down from another time?

Logically, he could only counter these contradictions and misgivings with the mask of the artist and so he let Rudolf M. Schindler speak for himself: "An architect is an artist. Architects must execute a different thing so that their buildings lose the background of those who built them; try and see what lies behind the shape of the building. That sounds abstract but it is really very simple."[1]

With his books under his arm and the writings of Ralph Waldo Emerson, Jean-Jacques Rousseau, and Henry David Thoreau in his head, Rudolf M. Schindler continued working as an architect until his death in 1953. A number of very beautiful houses forms an extraordinary oeuvre of far-reaching and still highly topical significance—this much Jeremy learned from a circle of young architects. Jeremy would have liked to find out whether the artist Rudolf M. Schindler ever enjoyed comparable times again after the happy years he spent with his friends at Kings Road, a period that did after all last an entire decade of a century shaped by Leonardo. But on that point, the experts are mum.

Nor was Jeremy able to answer Rebecca's last question. She wanted to know whether you can see the wide open sea, the Pacific Ocean, from the house in Kings Road, if ever she were to be a guest there. Instead of answering, he told her the story of the Japanese stonecutter or quite simply the story of the artist. As a good-bye present, Jeremy wanted to give Rebecca the book that contains this wonderful tale by Holland's great 19th-century writer, Multatuli. But she was already gone, having vanished as suddenly as she had appeared.

Later she did send a postcard from California, filled with the blue of sky and ocean; he was happy for her. But he had no desire to join her, for meanwhile he had found out, in his own way, almost everything about the house in Kings Road.

What ever moved Rimbaud to go into the desert? He now knew for certain: things that might as easily be found in the Bernese Oberland or in Brittany. But in order to see one of his all-time favorites, *L'entrée du Christ à Bruxelles* by James Ensor, Jeremy will not get around making the trip to California, because this masterwork has not left Malibu for years. The journey lies ahead, but so far he has been unable to make up his mind to go.

[1] (quoted from a lecture on "Architektur und Architekten," 1930, in
   Visionäre und Vertriebene, exh. cat., essay by Sarnitz, p.111, upper left)

Schindler Guide
Complete listing of all
existing buildings by R.M. Schindler

David Leclerc

Introduction

The following includes the presentation of 29 buildings by Rudolf Schindler located in the Los Angeles area. The selection has been made according to the importance of each project and its current condition. Some significant works, such as the Rodakiewicz House, have not been included in this selection, because they have been remodeled beyond recognition. Going on a Schindler tour of Los Angeles is a work of archeology. Very few buildings remain intact — most of them have suffered remodeling, the most common of which is the enclosure of decks, terraces, and balconies originally designed as outdoor living spaces.

Unlike modern architecture in Europe or on the East Coast, Schindler's buildings were almost never painted white. Schindler chose earth tones to blend 'organically' with the natural colors of the hillsides. Over the years, the natural and urban landscape surrounding these buildings has changed tremendously. What was once a dry, barren hillside might be built up and densely vegetated today, often blocking some of the original vistas. Downhill houses are generally very difficult to see from the street. Moreover, Schindler's inside-out design methodology makes understanding these buildings from the outside difficult, if not impossible. The current condition and accessibility of the buildings are indicated in the project descriptions and in the complete listing of existing works. Most houses are private residences, and the privacy of their inhabitants does not allow for public access. Leaving a note in the mail box or sending a letter stating an interest in visiting the house might help to obtain private appointments.

Unless otherwise stated, drawings and photographs have come from the Schindler Archives, Architectural Drawing Collection, University Art Museum, University of California, Santa Barbara. We are grateful to the staff at the Schindler Archives for their assistance. Many current owners of Schindler's houses have opened their homes to the author and therefore made this publication possible. All are sincerely thanked.

1 Schindler House

Residence for R. M. Schindler and Clyde Chace, 1921–1922
835 North Kings Road, West Hollywood

In his article 'Care of the Body', Schindler describes the house of the future: "Our rooms will descend close to the ground and the garden will become an integral part of the house. The distinction between the indoors and the out-of-doors will disappear. The walls will be few, thin and removable. All rooms will become parts of an organic unit instead of being small separate boxes with peep-holes."[1] The house, designed by Schindler as a 'cooperative dwelling' for his family and their friends, the Chaces, exemplifies these principles. Its innovative typology, combined with the application of utopian ideals, was remarkable at the time of its construction and contributed to the development of a uniquely Californian residential architecture. Originally considered radical and unconventional, the house is now recognized as one of the most important buildings in modern architecture.

Located on a large city lot, 100 by 200 feet (30 by 60 m), the house is set back from the street in the middle portion of the site but extends sideways almost to the property limits. The genius of the plan is in the integration of the building and the landscape. Schindler considered the entire lot as living space, divided into enclosed and open zones. The plan has a pinwheel configuration and is composed of four studios, a guest quarters, and a garage. Each pair of studios forms an 'L'

Construction work at the Schindler House, 1921/22

and opens through sliding canvas doors onto a patio used as an outdoor living room. The concrete floor and roof canopy extend two and a half feet (76 cm) onto the outdoor patio, creating a transitional zone between interior and exterior that is also used as a secondary circulation path between studios. Walls of shrubbery and bamboo extend the lines of the house into the landscape, protecting it from the street, insuring privacy on each patio, and articulating the garden into different functional zones.

When describing the 'architectural scheme' of the house, Schindler wrote: "Each room in the house represents a variation on one structural and architectural theme. This theme fulfills the basic requirements for a camper's shelter: a protected back, an open front, a fireplace, and roof. The shape of the rooms, their relation to the patios, and their alternating roof levels create an entirely new spatial interlocking between the interior and the garden." [2] The house is on one level, with the exception of the sleeping baskets on the roof. Two different ceiling heights are used to articulate the interior spaces, creating different zones within each room and providing a space for clerestory light to enter. While each person receives a large private studio for working,

Schindler House, aerial view

relaxing, or simply entertaining, each couple shares a common entrance hall, a bathroom, and a 'sleeping basket' on the roof to sleep in the open. A 'utility room' containing a kitchen and laundry equipment is used by all inhabitants in common and is located in the center of the house. The house sits on a flat concrete slab poured directly on the ground. Used both as the foundation and final floor, this avoided expensive excavation for a basement. The slab was also used as the surface for the on-site prefabrication of the walls: Tilt-up

Schindler House, front patio and the Chaces' room, 1953

Pauline Schindler's room after renovation, 1987

panels were cast on the slab and lifted up to create a solid back wall for each unit. The three-inch (7.6 cm) slot remaining in between was filled with concrete, frosted glass, or clear glass, providing three possible degrees of transparency. The rest of the structure is made of a light redwood frame infilled with different materials: clear glass, frosted glass, and Insulite, a rigid insulation board. "This house is a simple weave of a few structural materials which retain their natural color and texture throughout." [3]

Pauline Schindler's room, 1995

Pueblo Ribera Court
Vacation Houses for W. L. Lloyd, 1923–1925
230 Gravilla Street, La Jolla

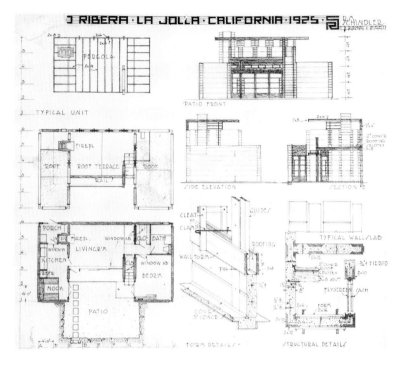

Schindler's interest in merging indoor and outdoor spaces, exemplified in his own house on Kings Road, is further explored in his first multi-dwelling complex, Pueblo Ribera Court, in La Jolla. The program called for 12 individual units on a sloping site facing the ocean, which were to serve as minimal shelter for an informal oceanside lifestyle.

The site plan is organized so that the back wall of one unit also forms the garden enclosure for its neighbor, generating a series of private garden courts. This theme is repeated with variations throughout the scheme, creating a great variety of outdoor spaces. The site is divided by a public alley which accesses three garage buildings, while private walkways lead to the entrance of each unit.

Pueblo Ribera Court, patio elevation of a unit with roof terrace, 1941

Pueblo Ribera Court, street front, 1925

The overall feeling of the plan is organic and random, but it is the product of a highly hierarchical circulation diagram and careful space planning to make each unit as private as possible. Each U-shaped unit is made up of two lateral masses framing a central living area. This opens onto a private garden area used as an outdoor living room. The roof terrace, covered with a suspended trellis, is accessed by an outdoor stairway and used as a living and sleeping space and for viewing the ocean.

The ingenuity of Schindler's space-planning is reinforced by the use of innovative construction techniques. Schindler utilized here, for the first time, his 'slab-cast wall' technique. The concrete wall was cast in 16-inch (40 cm) horizontal bands, the wood plank framework being raised after each cast, leaving a thin, recessed shadow line between them. These horizontal lines match the window mullions and redwood siding to visually and proportionally unite the materials. Over the years, the project has been severely altered. Some units were destroyed by fire. Others have been remodeled beyond recognition. Only a few remain in fair condition, but their roof trellises have been removed.

Pueblo Ribera Court, street front, 1941

Residence for J.C. Packard, 1924

931 North Gainsborough Drive, South Pasadena

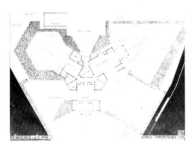

Packard House, view from the garden of the living room wing, ca. 1924

The concept of the Packard House was to configure the structure in such a way as to create several separate outdoor spaces that relate to the adjoining interiors. The flat triangular lot gave the house its unusual Y-shaped plan which divides the yard into six private gardens, each of which is assigned a specific use. The interior spaces are also organized according to the geometry of the plan: the main branch of the 'Y' contains the entry and the living room, whereas the smaller wings are for the parents' and the children's rooms. Intermediate zones are used for circulation, outdoor porches, and servant's quarters.

Local design restrictions required a pitched roof. Schindler responded by covering the living room wing with a steep gable roof, wrapped with overlapping sheets of asphalt roll roofing, while the rest of the house has a flat roof. Although some of the details, such as the window mullions and the roof shape, are reminiscent of the work of Frank Lloyd Wright, the plan clearly differs from Wright's spatial ideas. The fireplace, for example, no longer marks the center of the house. Instead, Schindler placed the kitchen in the triangular space at the intersection of the three wings, making it the 'heart' of the house. Continuing his experiments with concrete, Schindler built the walls out of reinforced concrete studs connected to two thin layers of gunnite, a sprayed-on concrete applied over wire mesh, the air space between the two layers providing a good moisture barrier and efficient insulation. The concrete walls extend to door height, with the entire upper structure and roof built out of wood. Looking at period photographs, the rather dark living room nave conveys a rustic atmosphere that recalls the work of the early modernist California architect Bernard Maybeck.

Interior view of living room, ca. 1924

Residence for J.E. How, 1925
2422 Silver Ridge Avenue, Los Angeles (Silverlake area)

View of How House from down the hill, ca.1925

The How House represents a turning point in Schindler's early work in terms of the manipulation of space. Schindler's interest in geometry and proportion as a generator of space is combined with a sensitive use of materials. Located on a ridge with views in two directions–the Los Angeles River Valley to the east and Silverlake to the west–the house faces the view like the bow of a boat pointing towards the horizon. The steep slope of the site required a confined footprint. The house is therefore made up of two structures: the lower portion is a square concrete base set at a 45-degree angle to the slope and built with the 'slab-cast' technique used at Pueblo Ribera, while the upper portion is a light wood frame. The sleeping areas and the garage are housed in the base. The main living spaces are located on the upper level and are organized in an L-shaped plan around a corner terrace. Two wings extend beyond the base toward the street and provide the main entrances to the house.

The spatial experience of the house is intimately related to the geometry out of which it has grown. The tall square volume of the living room dominates the center of the composition and opens to the two opposite outlooks through large corner windows. It thus emphasizes the diagonal axis around which the plan is symetrically organized and visually reunites the distant hori-

How House, 1995

Rear view, 1995

zons that the house has interrupted by its very presence on the hilltop. The interior space is the result of a complex layering process. Schindler describes it as follows: "The arrangement of the rooms features the two outlooks which the location offered. The rooms form a series of right angle shapes placed above each other and facing alternatingly north and south. This scheme provides sufficient terraces necessary for outdoor life. The angles are further placed in such a way as to frame an open shaft between them. This shaft illuminates the hall downstairs. It affords a direct view from the lowest floor to the highest ceiling of the living room, thus emphasizing the spatial unity of the structure." [4]

The light, wooden upper structure of the house is woven carefully into the massive concrete base, interlocking the two systems. The strong contrast between the materials is mitigated by Schindler's skill at uniting them visually. The 16-inch (40 cm) module of the 'slab-cast' wall matches the horizontal 'drip strips' used both as a batten for the redwood siding and as a mullion for

View of the entry, 1995

View of the living room, 1995

the glazing of the windows, creating a continuous pattern of horizontal lines throughout the structure. "This horizontal stratification ... is used as a contrast to the towering eucalyptus trees,"[5] Schindler said. The house has been restored by its current owner and is today a unique example of Schindler's early work.

12 Wading Pool and Pergola for A. Barnsdall, 1925
Barnsdall Park, Olive Hill, Los Angeles
(Corner of Hollywood Blvd. and Vermont Ave.)

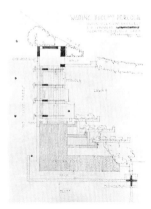

Downhill view of Wading Pool and Pergola, 1925

In 1920, while working for Frank Lloyd Wright at Taliesin East, Schindler was sent to Los Angeles to supervise the construction of Wright's projects for Aline Barnsdall on Olive Hill (known today as Barnsdall Park). While Wright exerted a seminal influence on Schindler's architectural ideas, Schindler's influence on Wright's designs for Olive Hill is more difficult to assess. Historians have recently argued Schindler's paternity of, for example, the Director's Residence located at the entrance to the park. After falling out with Wright, Aline Barnsdall commissioned Schindler, who had recently opened his own bureau, to work on several projects: the remodeling of a bedroom and a bathroom at the upper level of Hollyhock House (1924–25), followed by an extensive remodeling of Residence B — originally designed by Wright as a guest house — and resided in by Barnsdall after she donated the main house to the City of Los Angeles in 1927. (Residence B was destroyed by fire in 1954).

A smaller project, the Wading Pool and Pergola, were designed in 1925 by Schindler and the young Richard Neutra, who had recently arrived in Los Angeles. They are located on the west side of the hill and are in very poor condition. Schindler used the left-over concrete blocks and foundation intended for one of Wright's unbuilt projects and turned the site, which overlooks the city, into a small garden arranged around the pergola and wading pool. The sculptural arrangement of volumes, columns, and cantilevered wood beams stepped down the hillside is a moving testimony to Schindler's sensitivity to the site, and his mastery in the articulation of primary architectonic elements. (Accessible to the public).

Beach House for P. Lovell, 1925–1926
1242 Ocean Avenue, Newport Beach

View of Lovell Beach House from the beach, 1947

The Lovell Beach House, a summer residence for a well-known physician, is a pivotal work in Schindler's architectural development. Its complexity results from the intertwining of several different concerns: Schindler's growing interest in site-specific structural design, his emerging vocabulary of 'space forms', and his belief in architecture as a vehicle to change people's behavior. Based on a new and unconventional set of architectural and social ideas, the house was designed to promote the healthy and informal way of life espoused by Dr. Lovell. Located on the Balboa peninsula in Newport Beach, on a lot facing the beach, the house is elevated on piers to provide the living spaces with an unobstructed view of the ocean, and to give it some privacy from the public boardwalk. This also frees a small lot for an outdoor covered living space, complete with its own fireplace. "The motif used in elevating the house was suggested by the pile structure indigeneous to all beaches,"[6] wrote Schindler. The house is organized around a two-story, large informal room which opens to the ocean view through a finely articulated glass facade. The second floor, cantilevering into this volume, forms a balcony leading to four individual dressing rooms and sleeping porches beyond. The roof is used as a terrace, with a portion of it partitioned off for private sunbathing. While the street facade emphasizes the sequence of five concrete frames moving toward the ocean, the beach facade simply exposes the last frame, thus revealing the building's sectional idea. For the first time, Schindler made a clear distinction between structure and enclosure. The concrete frames were cast in place with a single reusable form; the walls, made of metal lath and cement plaster, are non-structural and simply suspended from the frames. The repetition of the frames is countered by the formal versatility of the enclosure and its intense articulation. The Lovell Beach House is one of Schindler's most controversial projects. While historians have often insisted on the ambiguity and contradictions which characterize the project, today it is considered one of the most important buildings of the Modern Movement. Its rejection from the International Style exhibition,[7] more than any other event, led to Schindler's marginalized status in the history of modern architecture.

Interior view of the two-story living room, 1926

15 Manola Court, Apartment Building for H. Sachs, 1926–1940

1811-1830 Edgecliff Drive, Los Angeles (Silverlake area)

Following the financial and technical problems encountered with the use of concrete in his earlier projects, Schindler was forced to abandon this modernist material in favor of the indigeneous wood frame construction with a stucco

Entry court on Edgecliff Drive, 1940s

View of the downhill facade, 1938
(as after first construction phase, 1926–1928)

skin. Although Schindler had previously described this system as "an inorganic, unelastic plaster slab supported by means of an organic swelling and shrinking skeleton,"[8] it suprisingly fulfilled his prediction, stated in his 1913 manifesto written in Vienna, of an architecture no longer concerned with structure but primarily with space.

The Sachs Apartments reveal a new language focused on the manipulation of volumes and a poetic use of common materials, but the most innovative aspect of this project remains its remarkable massing.

The site is a steep hillside, with a view facing west to the Hollywood Hills, bounded by streets at the top and bottom. In the first phase of the project, built between 1926 and 1928, residential units were organized along a stepped public walkway which divides the lot down the center and connects the two streets. At the top of the site, a U-shaped building, placed around a sunken entry court, houses larger apartments and a two-story studio. The profile of the building is kept low on the street side to match the residential scale of the surroundings, but its downhill facade is dramatic, extending over three stories and taking full advantage of the view. Below, smaller apartments built on top

View of entrance and stairs, 1995   *Sachs Apartments, 1995*

of parking garages are stepped down the hillside. An additional building with four apartments was added on the adjacent lot in 1939.

Schindler uses large window openings to break up the scale of the facade. He extends the window mullions into the stucco wall, creating a pattern of vertical wood battens which connect the windows and emphasize the verticality of the facade. Vegetation was intended to grow from built-in planters, further integrating building and landscape. The Sachs Apartments reveal the possibility of providing a dense urban fabric without compromising the assets of the 'American Dream': because each apartment has a separate outdoor entrance, each one seems as private as an individual home. Schindler created a building that is both urban in its massing, yet organic in its sensitivity to the hillside site.

6 Furnishings and Remodeling of Residence for S. Freeman, 1928, 1938, and 1953

1962 Glencoe Way, Los Angeles (Hollywood Hills area)

View of the living room, ca.1950

The most fascinating aspect of Schindler's remodeling of the Freeman House is the juxtaposition of his furniture design with Frank Lloyd Wright's architecture. The overlapping of these two languages of design creates a fascinating dialogue throughout the house.

Following the completion of the house—and after great difficulty between the architect and the client—the Freemans hired Schindler to design furniture and to remodel the kitchen and the bedroom area downstairs. The stiffness of Wright's original furnishings was inappropriate for the relaxed social life of this intellectual couple. Schindler designed each piece of furniture as a site-specific response to its location in the house. His built-in furniture, such as the bookshelves in the northwest corner of the living room, scrupulously respects Wright's textile block wall and its proportional grid. However, when the furniture extends into the room, as is the case with the two sofas in the living room, it reiterates Schindler's spatial ideas and architectural language.

In Harriet Freeman's bedroom, Schindler designed several sculptural pieces of cabinetry. In an intensively asymmetrical manner, these pieces contrast strongly with Wright's architecture. Only when opened out and unfolded into the room do these containers reveal their hidden contents. The static objects suddenly become animated—volumes pivot, panels unfold, and secret drawers slide, reminiscent of the ingenuity of the old traveling trunk. Made out of birch plywood, the smooth surfaces and golden color of the furniture con-

trast with the dark and rough texture of the textile block. The simplicity, inventiveness, and formal versatility of Schindler's interventions, within the special atmosphere of Wright's architecture, have the strength of a manifesto.

(Guided tours: Saturday at 2 pm and 4 pm)

View of the living room, 1995

Summer Residence for C.H. Wolfe, 1928–1929
Old Stage Road, Avalon, Catalina Island

Wolfe House, view of the downhill facade, 1931

Described by Schindler as "a composition of space units to float above the hill,"[9] the Wolfe House, a summer residence on Catalina Island, is the paradigm of Schindler's hillside house. The location of the house, on a steep hillside overlooking the bay of Avalon to the south and the Pacific Ocean to the east, is spectacular. The clients, Ethel and Charles Wolfe, had established a school of costume design in downtown Los Angeles, and looked upon Schindler's architecture as a way to promote the modernity of their institution. Their summer house was to be a rendezvous for their students during the summer months. Dedicated to Southern California's informal beach life, the program called for three independent apartments: one for the Wolfes, one for their guests, and one for staff.

The house is raised above the ground, avoiding expensive excavations and retaining walls. However, its cascading composition carefully follows the natural contour of the site, thus appearing like an abstraction of the hillside itself. The absence of outdoor gardens is compensated by large roof terraces for each apartment, created by stepping back each level. Each floor is organized according to the location of its entrance from the stepped walkway which wraps around the building and connects to the street above. Living rooms open onto the terraces which are protected on each side by solid volumes that create privacy from the adjacent lots. A partly covered roof terrace, with its own outdoor fireplace, is located on top of the building and is accessed by a ramp from the owners' apartment.

An interesting feature of this house, hardly visible from the outside, is its clever sectional trick: by manipulating the ceiling heights along the western facade, an additional mezzanine level has been 'shoe-horned' inbetween the guest quarters and the main apartment, for use as a single-car garage. The owners' bedroom, located over the garage, is consequently four feet (122 cm) higher than the living room. This change of level creates a spatial interplay and becomes the theme for an elaborate composition of built-in furniture.

Schindler also continued to pursue his experiments with new building materials. Here, the house is built with a typical wood frame with stucco, but Schindler used a steel deck for the floors with a poured-on, thin concrete layer. The corrugated metal, left exposed on the ceilings, was painted a dull gold. Today, the house is in poor condition and needs extensive restoration.

Residence for D. Grokowski, 1928
816 Bonita Drive, South Pasadena

View of Grokowski House with the roof terrace, 1928

The modest Grokowski House represents Schindler's emerging awareness of the potential offered by the wood frame covered with a stucco 'skin', and the possibility of adapting this construction system to his own spatial language.

Located on a small lot in South Pasadena, Schindler uses the sloping site to his advantage. The garage, placed between the house and the street, provides a roof terrace for the living room above. A stepped walkway, running along the side of the building, leads to the main entrance located at the back. Inside, a double-height living room is intersected by a bedroom loft space. Schindler brings his visitor directly into the vertical, double-height volume and uses the intimate area below the loft for the fireplace.

The plan, almost square at the entrance level, becomes highly articulated on the second floor as rooms are allowed to project out of the confines of the box. Various roof levels articulate the interior space and bring natural light into unexpected areas. To avoid the leaks inherent in a flat roof, Schindler introduced a series of gabled roofs to improve water drainage, while keeping their shallow slopes recessed from the facade, so as to give the appearance of a flat roof when viewed from the street. In addition to his plentiful use of natural light, Schindler continued his experiments with artificial light. By simply placing light bulbs in the spaces between the wall studs and covering them with frosted glass on both sides, he created built-in fixtures which glow simultaneously on the inside and the outside of the house. This enhances the reversible quality of his new 'skin design', with which the continuity of surfaces and finishes from the inside to the outside has the quality of erasing the boundaries between the two.

View of the interior and loft, 1995

Front view, 1995

13 Residence for R. F. Elliot, 1930
4237 Newdale Drive, Los Angeles (Los Feliz area)

Although the original massing of the house was altered with the addition of a studio in front, designed by Schindler in 1939, the Elliot House remains one of Schindler's greatest hillside designs. The house, modest in size and surprisingly compact on the site, exemplifies Schindler's elaborate articulation of the enclosure and interior spatial sequence. Located on an uphill site in the foothills of Los Feliz, the house is placed near the top of the lot with a small garden

View of Elliot House from downhill, 1939

behind it. Its orientation ignores both the street and the property lines, to respond exclusively to the topography and views. The garage acts as a marker to announce the presence of the house from the street. Similar to the Wolfe House, the building is raised above the ground, avoiding expensive excavations, and its volumes are stepped along the natural grade. Three functional zones parallel the contour of the land: the sleeping area and the entry hall are at the lower level, and the living area is upstairs. The extruded section of the living area opens out onto the garden at the rear and a roof terrace over the bedroom at the front.

By expanding the small entry hall into the living room above, Schindler introduces a two-story vertical space in the center of the house, filled with natural light. Schindler is now fully aware of the formal flexibility provided by wood-frame construction, articulating walls and ceilings to create deep spaces for outdoor planters and built-in furniture. The roof is stepped down towards the rear patio, forming an intimate area around the fireplace.

View from the entrance hall into the living room above, ca. 1986

The most original feature of the house is its trellis, which wraps around the living room and is duplicated at street level around the garage. Schindler described it as a 'hood' to shield the living spaces from the adjacent properties. Although he conceived the house as an abstract object floating above the sloping site, he also envisioned how vegetation would grow, and how the building would blend with the planted hillside. Today, the house is in poor condition and has structural problems. It is in need of restoration.

Residence for W. E. Oliver, 1933–1934

2236 Micheltorena Avenue, Los Angeles (Silverlake area)

View of Oliver House, 1933

The ambiguous, almost hybrid nature of the Oliver House is unique in Schindler's career. More than any other house, this building illustrates Schindler's ability to express and simultaneously resolve the tension between several contradictory architectural intentions. Here, 'space architecture' had to meet local design requirements which stipulated a pitched roof.

Located in the exclusive upper terraces of the hills surrounding Silverlake, the L-shaped house is built on the hilltop, with the garage below at street level. It is turned 45 degrees to the street to take advantage of splendid views of the ocean, the lake, and the San Gabriel mountains. The plan looks as if it has been 'cut off' at its extremities in order to fit within the property limits. The living area is organized in one wing, and the bedrooms are in the other. The children's quarters can be reached by an outdoor porch from the parents' bedroom. Another room was planned above the children's but was never built. Instead, a roof terrace, accessible by an outdoor stairway, provides spectacular views over the surrounding area. The most unusual aspect of the house is its roof design: the street facade presents a skillfully articulated 'modernist' box which, seemingly, has a flat roof while, in reality, the gable roof is fully exposed on the patio elevation and floats above the house like an umbrella. This kind of ambiguity, which would have been denounced as an anathema by followers of modern architecture in Europe, is used by Schindler to create an element of surprise. While the roof, viewed from the outside, seems to visually complete the flat top of the hill, its complex shape reinforces the sense of spatial continuity throughout the interior, providing a very sculptural quality to the rooms underneath.

View of the living room, 1930s

3 Residence for J.J. Buck, 1934

5958 Eighth Street, Los Angeles
(Corner of Eighth Street and Genesee Avenue)

RESIDENCE OF:
MR. & MRS. J. J. BUCK
LOS ANGELES, CALIF.
R. M. SCHINDLER, ARCHITECT
1 9 3 4

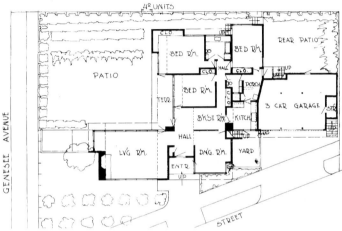

Located on a flat corner lot, in a typical residential neighborhood of Los Angeles, the Buck House is surrounded by single-family homes designed in historic, Revival styles. Schindler's abstract architectural composition seems alien in its environment, although it preceded most of these pastiches.

The house is carefully articulated to create two private outdoor living spaces protected from the street. The main residence is organized on one level, forming an L-shape around a secluded patio while a one bedroom rental apartment, located above the three-car garage, opens onto its own private courtyard. The skillfully articulated street facade reveals Schindler's mastery

View of Buck House from Genesee Avenue, 1934

View of the living room, 1976

for shaping space. The sculptural composition of volumes is emphasized by their orientation along the street at a slight angle. Windows are kept high to shield the living spaces from the street, while the house is fully open onto the patio through an uninterrupted glass facade.

The flatness of the site is emphasized by the organization of the main house on one level. The variation of ceiling height becomes Schindler's means to articulate the interior space and allow light to enter through clerestory windows, even in the most secluded areas of the plan. The building seems to be made from one single expanse of material which has been folded to form enclosed spaces, thus creating a great sense of continuity between vertical and horizontal surfaces. Schindler further erases the distinction between indoor and outdoor spaces by unifying interior and exterior surfaces: the architectural envelope is treated like a reversible skin. The small rental

View of Buck House, 1995

View from the yard onto the apartment terrace, 1995

apartment is a fine example of Schindler's ability to make a space seem larger than it is. He achieves this by controlling the views through a careful orchestration of windows and extending the visual space of the apartment beyond its physical enclosure. Experiencing this house leaves one with the feeling of living in pure light.

Residence for E. Van Patten, 1934–1935

2320 Moreno Drive, Los Angeles (Silverlake area)

The Van Patten House is an original response to the downhill site conditions that generated so many of Schindler's great houses in the 1930s. The plan is based on the transcription of a diagram sketch made by Schindler, showing the divergent views from the site towards the lake and the mountains. At street level, three attached garages covered with an unusual overlapping shed roof are placed behind one another, focusing the viewer's attention to the side where an entrance ramp is revealed. Behind the garages, and invisible from the street, is a two-story, Y-shaped house with a dramatic downhill facade embracing a view of Silverlake. The two orthogonal wings open towards the view with full-height corner glass facades, while the central axis is interrupted by a service core which blocks an undesirable view facing the house. The main living area and the master bedroom are at street level under the roof canopy, and two guest bedrooms are on the lower floor. The slope of the inverted gable roof is repeated in the balconies and the ramp, creating a dynamic downhill facade which rises up in a counter motion. The house is conceived as an organism which embraces—rather than simply faces—the view, incorporating it into its internal spatial experience. It is clearly designed from the inside-out. Typical of Schindler's work of this period, the house seems an odd composition when viewed from the outside, while its logic is fully revealed on the inside: it can only be understood through actual experience and is indeed an enriching place in which to live.

The living room with view of Silverlake, 1930s

View of the downhill facade of Van Patten House, 1940

7 Duplex Residence for J. De Keyser, 1935

1911 Highland Avenue, Los Angeles (Hollywood Hills area)

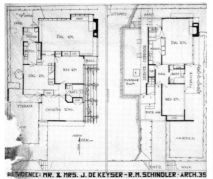

RESIDENCE: MR. & MRS. J. DE KEYSER - R.M. SCHINDLER · ARCH. 35

View of the downhill facade of De Keyser Duplex in 1935

As its current owner puts it, it is amazing how much architecture Schindler can make out of almost nothing: the De Keyser House was built for $2.00 a sq. ft. Perched on a hillside on the west side of Highland Avenue, just below Frank Lloyd Wright's Freeman House, the house was originally composed of two separate apartments. To minimize foundation cost, Schindler abandons his 'stepping' strategy and stacks the units on top of each other, generating a vertical composition on the slope. An outdoor entrance hall, built into a recess on the side of the building, provides separate access to each unit. The roof, covered with overlapping bands of asphalt roll-roofing, is visually detached from the stucco box by windows. The same roofing material is used on some parts of the facade, suggesting that the roof is folded over. The upper apartment is articulated in two interlocking volumes, one for living, the other for sleeping. Each room has direct access to an outdoor space, whether it is the rear patio, a covered deck, or a corner balcony. Inside the living room, Schindler, once again, created an element of surprise: the roof, which appears flat from downhill, is in reality a sloping shed roof hidden behind a large fascia on the front elevation. Clerestory windows bathe the exposed rafters and

R.M. Schindler: Presentation drawing of the downhill facade, 1935

View of the downhill facade, 1995

plywood ceiling in warm, southern light. By simply playing with different materials and built-in furniture, Schindler transforms the interior space into a three-dimensional collage of plywood, plaster, and glass. The original color scheme of the house was derived from the natural colors of the eucalyptus found on the site: the light tan of the upper layer of the bark for the stucco, the brown-red of the inner layer of the bark for the window trims, the green of the leaves for the roofing material.

View of the living room, 1995

2100 Kenilworth Avenue, Los Angeles (Silverlake area)

View of the downhill facade of Walker House, 1937–1938

Schindler describes three different 'form schemes' for the hillside houses: "balancing above the hill, cascading down with the slope, and rising up in a counter motion."[10] While the Van Patten House illustrates the third category, the Walker House exemplifies the second. Typical of Schindler's downhill designs, the street elevation is kept low while the house expands to the maximum on the downhill side and takes full advantage of the view. A long clerestory window detaches the roof plane from the volumes housing the garage and the maid's quarters on the street side. Shielded behind them, the main living area, organized around a core formed by the fireplace and the kitchen, is fully open to the view; the bedrooms and a playroom occupy the lower level. The location of the stairs along a large window on the side facade makes one constantly aware of living on a steep slope. This feeling is reinforced by the sloping ceiling of the living room and its complex geometry, which follows the topography of the hillside. The roof canopy is further lifted from the wall, allowing clerestory light into the space.

The articulated base of the building is one of its best-known features. A row of eight concrete columns elevates the volume of the house while creating a porch underneath it. The trellis, which cantilevers from this structure, expands on the side to become an overhanging balcony for one of the bedrooms. Views are framed in sensitive ways, giving each room a different relationship to the outside: some open widely onto outdoor terraces while others are closed up, barely lit by clerestory light. The house is simultaneously introverted and in harmony with the surrounding natural and urban environment.

Residence for Victoria McAlmon, 1935

2717-2721 Waverly Drive, Los Angeles (Silverlake area)

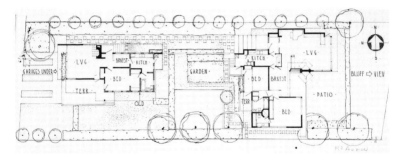

The McAlmon House is one of the most sculptural pieces of architecture Schindler ever produced. The intensely articulated body of the main house is set on a hilltop, like a sculpture on a pedestal, in a precarious state of balance. Rather than using a 'tabula rasa' approach, Schindler took advantage of an existing bungalow, located on the street, and remodeled it as a prelude to the main house above. He wrapped the existing structure in his vocabulary of space-forms, with the exception of the original pitched roof, which emerges like a reminder of a past life. The asymmetrical street facade of the bungalow focuses the viewer's attention to the side, where the walkway leading to the main house is located. A skillfully calculated distance separates the two structures. Climbing up the hill, along the side wall of the bungalow, one experiences Schindler's ability to articulate the house so that it responds to the visitor's approach: the volume of the kitchen, detached from the roof plane, projects out to reinforce the reading of an adjacent recess which is used as an entrance porch. This counter movement, pulled-out vs. pushed-in, engages the visitor with the composition while terminating the carefully controlled axis of the approach. Once inside, the procession has come to an end, and now the goal of 'space architecture' is to provide a place for human life. The interior space, subtly articulated on two different levels to differentiate day and night activities, is calm in comparison with the dramatic sequence of entry, suggesting a sense of settlement. The main living area, organized around an outdoor breakfast room, opens up to the backyard and enjoys a magnificent view of the Los Angeles River Valley.

View of the front facade, 1933–37

View of the living room, 1930s

Residence for C.C. Fitzpatrick, 1936
8078 Woodrow Wilson Drive, Los Angeles (Hollywood Hills area)

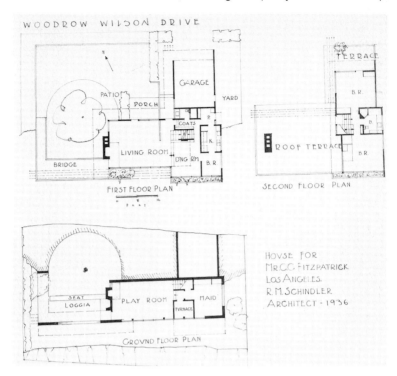

Schindler often stated his disagreement with the so-called 'functionalists' and the ideas of the International Style. With the Fitzpatrick House he nonetheless came very close to the imagery promoted by them. Driving up Laurel Canyon, just before reaching Mulholland Drive, one can see the stretched facade of the

View of Fitzpatrick House from Laurel Canyon Drive, 1937–38

View of the living room, 1937–38

house — now much altered — on the uphill side of the road, behind a screen of eucalyptus trees. Although the area behind the house is basically flat, the building is located on the edge of the cliff in order to get the best views of the canyon. The plan is a simple 'L' shape. The main living space faces the view, while the garage and the sleeping area are located in a two-story wing perpendicular to it. A lower level, which takes advantage of the slope at the edge of the property, houses a playroom and maid's quarters. Designed to emphasize the presence of the building along the road, the canyon facade extends beyond the house itself to a free-standing wall, with a large opening for an outdoor loggia behind it. A bridge connecting the living room to the garden forms a canopy above. The stepped volumetry of the building conveys a sense of motion while dissolving gradually into the landscape. Floors and roof planes extend beyond the facade to protect the glass walls from the southern sun. The strong shadows cast by these projections reinforce a sense of horizontality behind the vertical lines of the trees. The asymmetry of the overall composition is carried into the 'shaping' of the interior spaces and the design of the built-in furniture.

16 Apartment Building for A. Bubeshko, 1938 and 1941
2036 Griffith Park Boulevard, Los Angeles (Silverlake area)

Schindler's idea to make the building an abstraction of the hillside is once again reiterated in this multi-family dwelling complex. The building is located on an uphill site in Silverlake. The lot is cut at a 45-degree angle at the bottom by Griffith Park Boulevard. A series of parallel walls defines the edge of the street and creates partitions between the garages. Several layers of thick roof canopies stacked on top of each other slide into the hillside, like drawers. This stepping composition breaks down the scale of the building and integrates it into the hillside, while providing each unit with a large private roof terrace

Front view of Bubeshko Apartments with entrance and steps

on top of the apartment below. Schindler's 'pancake' strategy is clearly visible on the north facade, where each 'spatial layer' is separated from the one below by a continuous row of windows or simply differentiated by cantilevering out. Stepped walkways, running along the property lines, are protected by these overhanging roof canopies, allowing access to the apartments on either side. Each unit has its own outdoor entrance porch, making it as private as an individual home. Living rooms open onto roof terraces and the outside of the lot, while bedrooms and service areas are mainly organized along a central alley.

Inside, the rooms are highly articulated with elaborate built-in furniture. By using different finishing materials, Schindler emphasizes the continuity between vertical and horizontal planes: plain sheets of plywood alternate with a ribbed pattern of board and batten, plastered walls, and glass, thus transforming the room into a three-dimensional 'collage'.

The building is rational and efficient in its organization, without being monotonous or repetitive. On the contrary, the diversity of exterior spaces and interior treatments gives each unit its own identity.

View of Bubeshko Apartments from Griffith Park Boulevard, 1941

View of the living room of an apartment with roof terrace, 1941

19 Residence for G.C. Wilson, 1935–1939
2090 Redcliff Street, Los Angeles (Silverlake area)

The Wilson House is located on a downhill lot with a magnificent view of Silverlake. The garage acts as a buffer along the street and is placed parallel to the curb, while the house, attached to the back of the garage, stands at an angle to get the best views of the lake. The house is entered at its highest level, with the living areas located at street level. The bedrooms and private rooms are further down the slope. The dramatic three-story downhill facade was originally symmetrical (before several remodelings by Schindler) and rested on a base which extended on the north side, providing a terrace for the lower level. This symmetrical condition was transformed by Schindler's manipulation of the section: each floor

View of Wilson House from downhill, 1995

projects above the lower one, creating a triple cantilevered facade which culminates in a dynamic tapered roof plane, suggesting a sense of motion toward the view. The roof canopy, in the shape of a butterfly, allows clerestory light to enter from above the garage into the dining room. The living room was originally flanked on both sides by small symmetrical balconies, like saddle bags (the one on the north side is now a large terrace). The stairs act as a pivot between the garage and the house, and generate a complex sequence of hallways and landings which play against the double orientation of the plan. As in many other houses, the richness of the interior space is further enhanced by Schindler's ability to draw the outdoor world in.

View of the living room, 1995

90

Apartment Building for S.T. Falk, 1939–1940

3631 Carnation Avenue, Los Angeles (Silverlake area)

View of Falk Apartments from Carnation Avenue, 1947

The Falk Apartments are a striking example of Schindler's ability to create four interlocking living units on a difficult site without compromising any of the principles developed in his single-family houses. The triangular shape of the lot, located on a hillside overlooking Hollywood, generated the complex massing of the project. Playing with an overlay of two grids, Schindler creates a composition of volumes which twist and turn to take full advantage of the view. He further uses the garages to articulate the corner of the street, shielding the four apartments, and provides each unit with a private roof terrace. A small courtyard, accessed from the street by narrow passages, forms the intersection of these volumes. From this void the spatial complexity of the project can be fully experienced. The building is urban in that it respects the alignment of the street, and organic in that it recreates the hillside in a highly sculptural manner.

The penthouse offers a magnificent view over its surroundings. Housed under a heavy roof canopy, covered on the inside with a pattern of interlocking sheets of plywood, the main living area extends out at its two extremities onto two opposite outdoor spaces: a roof terrace overlooking the cityscape at one end and a densely planted private patio on the opposite side. Schindler also plays with visual transparency between rooms, creating a continuous spatial flow throughout the apartment. The variety of natural light entering the interior progressively dissolves the reading of the enclosure.

Page 92: Penthouse, view from the entrance hall up to the living room, 1947

Commercial Buildings for William Lingenbrink: Modern Creators, 1936–1938 and 1946

2

Corner of Holloway Drive and Palm Avenue, West Hollywood

Stores on Ventura Boulevard, 1939–1942

9

12634-12670 Ventura Boulevard, Studio City

View of Modern Creators Shop ca. 1940

Schindler designed and built a number of stores, offices, and restaurants in the course of his career. His most important commercial commissions, located in Hollywood, have been destroyed: the Sardi's Restaurant and Lindy's Restaurant, both of 1932–34. Very few examples of Schindler's commercial architecture remain today in Los Angeles. Two complexes of stores designed for a developer and friend, William Lingenbrink, have sustained severe damage from successive remodelings, but their spirit is nonetheless alive.

At the Modern Creators, Schindler respects the original lot subdivision and breaks down the complex into smaller buildings, each with its own identity, thereby acknowledging the typical urban landscape along commercial strips. The same principles found in his residential projects apply to this commercial building—roofs are lifted and detached from the wall, derestory windows bring natural light to areas that usually remain dark, and display windows become volumes of glass projected out and angled to catch the driver's or pedestrian's attention. Special care is given to make signs and lighting an integral part of the architecture. Schindler's ideas of 'space architecture' are here adapted to commercial use. The Lingenbrink Shops on Ventura Boulevard are Schindler's interpretation of the now common typology of the 'mini-mall'. Rather than placing all the stores in one single building, Schindler designed each one as a variation on a theme. Visibility for each shop is heightened by staggering the facade. Flat roofs fold vertically to generate a series of blank walls, perpendicular to the street, for sign display, thus giving the building its jagged skyline. Three materials—flagstone, stucco, and glass—create a continuous pattern of interlocking forms throughout the stores' facades, unifying the overall complex. In this project, Schindler once again reveals his interest in reflecting the diversity and heterogeneity of the urban landscape in his architecture.

Interior view, 1938

4 Apartment Building for Pearl Mackey, 1939

1137 South Cochran Avenue, Los Angeles

View of Mackey Apartments from Cochran Avenue

The Mackey Apartment Building is another interesting example of Schindler's ability to transform the most common typology of apartment building found in the Los Angeles area and adapt it with his own spatial language. The building is located on a flat lot in a typical residential neighborhood of Los Angeles. Like all the other apartment buildings on this street, it has a front yard and a driveway on the side which accesses a garage court located at the back. This layout, imposed by zoning, prescribes any private outdoor living spaces around the building. Schindler reclaims the front yard by creating two small private gardens for the ground floor units. A fence is created out of a low

Interior view of penthouse

stucco band, lifted off the ground, combined with high shrubbery which thus ensures privacy from the street. The building is compact but nonetheless highly articulated. The coexistence of four living units is expressed by interlocking 'space forms' on the facade. Schindler further utilizes deep walls and recessed windows to break with the typical flat stucco facade, creating a dynamic and asymmetrical composition of strong volumetric presence. While the apartments are almost symmetrical on the ground floor, the introduction of a two-story volume for the owner's penthouse above dramatically changes the spatial organization of the upper floor and allows rear access to a roof terrace. Inside the apartments, partition walls are visually separated from the ceiling with glass panels, providing transparency between the rooms. In typical Schindler fashion, the roof is lowered in the center of the building to allow natural light to enter through clerestory windows into the most removed interior areas, thereby avoiding dark corners.

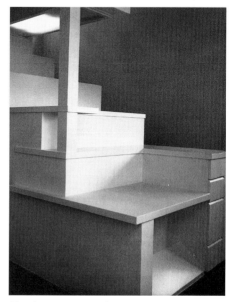
Penthouse, detail of built-in furniture

21 Residence for G. Droste, 1940
2035 Kenilworth Avenue, Los Angeles (Silverlake area)

Front view of Droste House, 1986

Schindler's projects from the 40s become increasingly subjective and more difficult to read from the exterior. The Droste House is clearly a transitional design that introduces his post-war period.

The house is located on an uphill lot with a view over Silverlake, at a sharp bend in the street. The difficult access to the site forced Schindler to dedicate the area in front of the house to parking and to raise the living space above.

The house is composed of two volumes organized parallel to the slope. The front is a three-story volume which houses a two-car garage at the bottom with a two-story living room on top. The living room opens laterally onto a terrace entrance on one-side and a patio on the other. The rest of the house is organized into a one-story volume attached to the back of the living room at its upper level. Although the separation of the living area on two different floors is a rather unusual layout for Schindler, he managed to create a spatial interplay between them: the dining room becomes a loft space overlooking the living room below.

The massiveness of the front contrasts with the modest and generic aspect of the rear elevation. A gable roof, which in typical Schindler fashion is invisible from the street, is used to reinforce the spatial continuity between the two volumes. Schindler adjusts the slope of the roof to introduce clerestory windows, bringing natural light to a dark corner or to frame some elements of the landscape outside: a small triangular opening placed under the gable end provides a glimpse of the eucalyptus trees up the hill.

Interior, with view of Silverlake, 1986

Bethlehem Baptist Church, 1944

4900 South Compton Avenue, Los Angeles (South Central area)

The Bethlehem Baptist Church is Schindler's only public building still standing and his sole church design. Located in South Central Los Angeles, on a corner lot, the L-shaped church defines the street edge along Compton Avenue and shields the lot behind it. A covered walkway connects the church to a secondary building located at the rear of the

View of Bethlehem Baptist Church from Compton Avenue, 1949

property, while creating an edge around a patio used for outdoor social gatherings. The roof terrace of the rear building was to be used as an open-air theatre with an outdoor stage.

Driving along Compton Avenue, the only identification of the building as a place of worship is a tower in the shape of a cross, which rises out of a skylight and hovers above the congregation. An exterior pattern of wide horizontal bands of stucco, repeated inside the church, conveys the impression that the building is covered with oversized lap-board siding, providing a monumental scale to this rather small church. This motif is also used to articulate several layers of the facade, creating a 'deep wall' that allows natural light to enter the interior laterally.

The L-shaped plan is organized to focus the congregation's attention on the corner, where the pulpit is located. Its diagonally symmetrical layout (recalling the How House designed twenty years earlier) is reinforced by

the exposed timber structure of the roof and the light penetrating from the skylight. While the facade on Compton Avenue closes off the church to protect it from the heavy traffic, giving the building its 'bunker' look, the radiant composition of the rear facade embraces the outdoor patio and invites the public to enter.

Interior view, 1949

11 Residence and Studio for M. Kallis, 1946

3580 Multiview Drive, Studio City

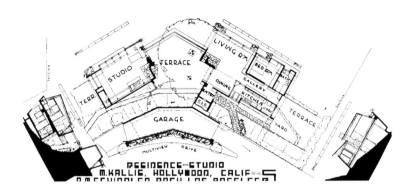

The Kallis House is a unique example of Schindler's late work: it combines a sensitive siting, an original 'extruded section' and a novel use of material. Set on a north-facing downhill lot with a view over Studio City and the San Fernando Valley, the house nestles into the hillside, its shape closely following the contour of the site. Its original design was a composition of two structures, carefully situated to preserve several oak trees. The first consisted of a painter's studio with a small, two-bedroom apartment beneath it; the second was a one-bedroom residence. The two buildings were linked by a corner terrace, built around the existing oak trees; from there, the magnificent view of the valley was framed by two massive stone fireplaces. The terrace has since been enclosed, unfortunately joining the two structures, but in a manner very sympathetic to the original materials and lines of the house.

The garage acts as a buffer along the street to protect the house and originally the terrace below. The linear plan of the house is composed of three parallel areas, each of which has a differentiated roof: the outer two slope inward, while the roof of the central corridor—designed as a gallery for the

View of Kallis House from the street, 1946

owners' collection of paintings and objects—is raised to allow light to enter through clerestory windows. As in many of Schindler's designs from the 1940s, the distinction between walls and ceilings tends to disappear. Here, Schindler tilts the walls to form one single entity with the sloping roof. On the inside, the exposed timber structure reinforces the continuity between the wall and the ceiling, while on the outside, siding made of large overlapping plywood boards gives the house the feeling of a hull.

View of Kallis House from below, 1995

Schindler's interest in using 'off the shelf' industrial materials is visible, once again, in this house. Parts of the building are wrapped with 'split-stake fencing', giving the facade an unusually irregular and rugged quality. The house appears as though it has been camouflaged to blend into the hillside.

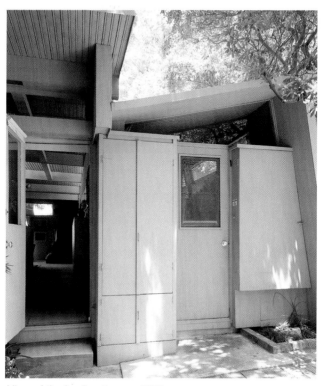

View of the back entrance, 1995

10 Laurelwood Apartments, 1946–1949
11833–11837 Laurelwood Drive, Studio City

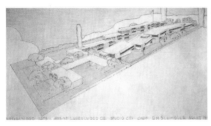

R.M. Schindler: Perspectival drawing of Laurelwood Apartments, 1946

View from Laurelwood Drive,1986

Schindler's post-war work is often understated and sometimes simply blends into the generic urban landscape of Los Angeles. The Laurelwood Apartments in Studio City could easily be taken for a standard apartment building of that period, if a closer look did not reveal Schindler's ingenuity in organizing twenty units on a narrow lot, making each of them as private as a house.

From the street the complex is hardly visible: a series of stepped terraces covered with dense vegetation forms an artificial hillside which blends into the residential neighborhood. Enclosed garage courts act as a buffer between the building and the street while forming a gateway to the central alley. Ten two-story units with an apartment on each floor are organized into two symmetrical rows separated by a central garden court. A staggered layout provides each unit with good views and multiple orientations. The layout is inverted on the hilltop so that the last two units can benefit from opposite views of the valley. Following the principle applied to his earlier hillside apartment buildings, Schindler steps the units upwards to follow the natural slope of the site. Ground floor units have private patios, while second floor apartments have a terrace on the roof of the adjacent unit. Outdoor staircases and private entrances give each tenant the feeling of living in his own house. Primarily oriented toward the outside of the lot, the small, two-bedroom apartments exemplify Schindler's skill at making a space feel bigger than it is, by using

glass partitions to provide visual transparency between rooms. The ceiling and the part of the wall above the door header are covered with stained wood in order to minimize the cost of painting.

View of the living room of a 2nd-floor apartment with roof terrace

Residence for E. Janson, 1948–1949

8704 Skyline Drive, Los Angeles (Hollywood Hills area)

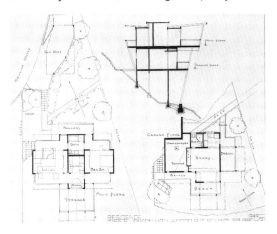

Schindler never came closer than with the Janson House to illustrating a recurring theme of his hillside designs—that of a tree house. The steepness of the site forced Schindler to abandon his usual strategy of stepping the volumes of the house down the slope in favor of stacking them on top of each other. The footprint of the building is therefore kept as small as possible to minimize the cost of the foundations, and the volumes are allowed to project over each other, giving the house the odd volumetry of an inverted pyramid. Schindler exploits the contrast between stucco surfaces and exposed timber. Decks and trellises cantilever out to provide ample outdoor living space. Angled wood supports, designed like huge ladders, connect these suspended platforms. All of these elements appear to be the product of ad-hoc design. Building materials and components remain in an 'as found' state, applied to, rather than absorbed into the house, creating an unusual collage aesthetic. The incompleteness and instability of the overall composition give the viewer the impression that the building 'just happened' and is still under construction. Unfortunately, this also had the disadvantage of inspiring the subsequent owner to 'complete' the design, enclosing and extending most of the terraces and trellises and enlarging the house beyond its original, tree-house-on-stilts appearance.

Side view of Janson House

5 Residence for A. Tischler, 1949–1950

175 Greenfield Avenue, Los Angeles (Westwood)

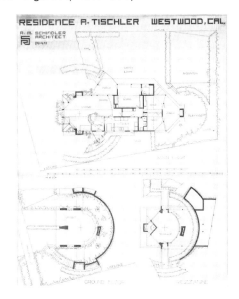

With the Tischler House, Schindler returns to his dream of a translucent house, originally conceived in his unrealized scheme for Alice Barnsdall in 1927. Viewed from the street, the house resembles the bow of a ship protruding from the trees. The vertical, highly sculptural street facade acts as a frontispiece, behind which the horizontal volume of the house is extended. The symmetry of the front elevation is broken by a complex orchestration of differentiated windows which wrap around the volume of the living room, subtly controlling the view.

In order to negotiate a very steep slope and avoid expensive excavations, the main house is elevated to form a bridge. While supported at the rear on the natural gradient, the longitudinal volume of the house, positioned along the edge of the lot, rests at the street front on a 'pier' composed of a two-car garage with a small, separate apartment stacked on top of it. As exempli-

View of Tischler House from Greenfield Avenue, 1995

Interior view with fireplace, 1995

fied by many of his houses from the 1940s, Schindler uses the roof as a device to unify the plan and provide spatial continuity between rooms. The steep gable roof is sheathed in blue corrugated fiberglass panels, forming a big tent under which the living spaces are freely arranged. Partition walls are only door height, with upper portions of glass, so that one can see through the entire volume without any obstruction. Although located in a densely populated residential neighborhood, the feeling inside of the house is that of floating in the trees in complete privacy and isolation.

Unfortunately, the fiberglass panels used for the roof were the source of numerous leaks, unbearable heat, and an unattractive blue light which flooded the interior. Today, the upper two-thirds of the panels have been doubled with plywood on the inside. The house has the distinction of being one of few Schindler houses that is still inhabited by its original owners. It was declared a historic cultural monument by the City of Los Angeles in 1991.

Interior view, 1995

Notes

1 R. M. Schindler, 'Care of the body—Shelter or Playground', published in *The Los Angeles Times*, May 2, 1926

2 R. M. Schindler, 'A Cooperative Dwelling', published in *T- Square*, February 1932

3 R. M. Schindler, 'A Cooperative Dwelling', published in *T- Square,* February 1932

4 R. M. Schindler, Description of the How House, from Schindler's building files, Schindler Archives, UCSB. Note that Schindler's indication of north and south are wrong. The two outlooks are in reality east and west. Same on the drawings.

5 R. M. Schindler, Description of the How House, from Schindler's building files, Schindler Archives, UCSB.

6 R. M. Schindler, Description of the How House, from Schindler's building files, Schindler Archives, UCSB.

7 Exhibition curated by P. Johnson and H. R. Hitchcock at the Museum of Modern Art, New York, 1932

8 R. M. Schindler's notes, quoted in Esther McCoy, *Five California Architects*, p.163.

9 R. M. Schindler, Description of the Wolfe House, from Schindler's building file, Schindler Archives, UCSB.

10 R. M. Schindler, Contribution for the *Directory of Contemporary Architecture* collected by the School of Architecture, University of Southern California, 1949

Complete list of Schindler buildings in the Los Angeles area

The following list includes all of the buildings in the Los Angeles area which are still standing. It does not include Schindler's remodeling of existing buildings. The list is in chronological order (the first date indicates the earliest design, and the second date refers to the year of completion). Buildings which are presented in this book are indicated in red.

Residence for R. M. Schindler and Clyde Chace, 1921–1922

835 N. Kings Rd., West Hollywood
Restored in 1987 to bring it back to the original design.
Very good condition. Open to the public.

Duplex Residence for O.S. Floren, 1922–1925

North side of Romaine St. between Harper St. and La Jolla St., West Hollywood
Remodeled. Spanish tiles were added on the parapet walls; the facade has been altered, but the original volumetry of the project still remains.

Duplex Residence for E.E. Lacey, 1922

830–832 Laguna Ave., Los Angeles
Remodeled.

Pueblo Ribera Court, Vacation Houses for W.L. Lloyd, 1923–1925

230 Gravilla St., La Jolla
The project has been severely altered. Some units were destroyed by fire. Others have been remodeled beyond recognition. Only a few remain in fair condition, but their roof trellises have been removed.

Residence for J.C. Packard 1924

931 North Gainsborough Dr., South Pasadena
Extensive remodeling. The roof, originally wrapped with industrial asphalt roll roofing, is now a picturesque gable covered with wood shingles. French glass doors were replaced by modern sliding doors. Porches have been enclosed, trellises were added, and an addition was built to the children's wing.

Residence for J.E. How, 1925

2422 Silver Ridge Ave., Los Angeles (Silverlake area)
Restored by current owners. Very good condition.

Wading pool and pergola for A. Barnsdall, 1925 (with R. Neutra)

Barnsdall Park, Olive Hill, Los Angeles. Entrance to the park off Hollywood Blvd. between Vermont Ave. and Edgemont St.
In very poor condition. Accessible to the public.

Beach House for P. Lovell, 1925–1926

(First sketch in 1922. Project for remodeling in 1947)

1242 Ocean Ave., Newport Beach

Good condition. At the client's request, the sleeping porch balcony and the open playground located underneath the house were enclosed by Schindler. The house's new color scheme, blue and brown, unfortunately has nothing to do with Schindler's original colors: natural white for the plaster, sand color for the stained wood and concrete frame.

Manola Court, Apartment Building for H. Sachs, 1926–1928 and 1934–1940

1811–1815 Edgecliff Dr., Los Angeles (Silverlake area)

Built in several phases. Good condition. Most of the original windows have been replaced by aluminum frames, and the vertical batten boards on the facade have been removed.

Residence for K. Sorg, 1926

530 S. Putney St., San Gabriel

Furnishings and Remodeling of Residence for S. Freeman, 1928, 1938 and 1953

1962 Glencoe Way, Los Angeles (Hollywood Hills area)

Exceptional ensemble of furniture designed for one of the most famous F.L. Wright 'textile block' houses. The house is owned by the University of Southern California. Tours of the house are held each Saturday at 2 pm and 4 pm. Reservations required for groups larger than 10. For information and reservations, call (213) 851-0671.

Summer Residence for C. H. Wolfe, 1928–1929

Old Stage Rd., Avalon, Catalina Island

In poor condition.

Residence for D. Grokowsky, 1928

816 Bonita Dr., South Pasadena

In poor condition. The original design is almost intact except for the screen wall of decorative concrete blocks on the terrace above the garage. The house is owned by Caltrans and is threatened to be destroyed by the construction of the Route 710 extension. Visits by appointment only. Call (213) 254-4277.

Cabins no.1 and no. 3 at Park Moderne, 1929 and 1938

Blackbird Way, Woodland Hills

Remodeled. (Not inspected).

Residence for R. F. Elliot, 1930

4237 Newdale Dr., Los Angeles (Los Feliz area)

In poor condition. Schindler added a studio for the Elliots in 1939 and attached it to the front facade below the bedrooms, altering the original design of the house. Most of the built-in furniture has been destroyed, and the kitchen was remodeled in 1954.

Residence for H. N. Van Koerber, 1931–1932

408 Monte d'Oro, Hollywood Riviera, Torrance
In the process of being remodeled or restored.

Residence for W. E. Oliver, 1933–1934

2236 Micheltorena Ave., Los Angeles (Silverlake area)
Intact. In good condition.

Cabin for A. Gisela Bennati, 1934–1937

Lake Arrowhead, Los Angeles County

Residence for J. J. Buck, 1934

5958 Eighth St., Los Angeles (corner of Eighth St. and Genesee Ave.)
Intact. In good condition.

Residence for Haines, 1934–1935

5112 Alishia Dr., Dana Point.

Residence for E. Van Patten 1934–1935

2320 Moreno Dr., Los Angeles (Silverlake area)
Remodeled. The three-car garage was converted into living space.
An addition has been built on the side of the house where the original entrance was located.

Residence for R. G. Walker, 1935–1936

2100 Kenilworth Ave., Los Angeles (Silverlake area)
Intact. Has suffered earthquake damage, but is in the process of being restored.

Duplex Residence for J. De Keyser, 1935

1911 Highland Ave., Los Angeles (Hollywood Hills area)
Intact. In the process of being restored.

Residence for Victoria McAlmon, 1935

2717-2721 Waverly Dr., Los Angeles (Silverlake area)
Intact. In good condition.

Residence for G. C. Wilson, 1935–1939

2090 Redcliff St., Los Angeles (Silverlake area)
The downhill facade is visible from Kenilworth Ave. down below.
In good condition. Some remodeling. The lower side terrace was enclosed; the living room balcony was enlarged into a terrace.
Visits by appointment only. Call (213) 661-9035.

Modern Creators, Commercial Building for W. Lingenbrink 1936–1938 and 1946

Corner of Holloway Dr. and Palm Ave., West Hollywood
Remodeled.

Residence for C.C. Fitzpatrick, 1936

8078 Woodrow Wilson Dr., Los Angeles (Hollywood Hills area)
Can be seen best from below on Laurel Canyon just before reaching Mulholland Drive.
Remodeled. The volumetry is still there, but the original glass facade on Laurel Canyon was closed off and replaced by smaller punched openings. The garage has been converted into living space and a carport has been added.

Residence for H. Rodakiewicz, 1937

9121 Alto Cedro Dr., Los Angeles
Extensively remodeled. Nothing is left of the original design.

Apartment Building for A. Bubeshko, 1938 and 1941

2036 Griffith Park Blvd., Los Angeles (Silverlake area)
Built in two phases. In good condition. Some minor remodeling on the facade.

Residence for M. Southall, 1938

1855 Park Dr., Los Angeles

Residence for S.N. Westby, 1938, 1939, 1944–1945, 1949

1805 N. Maltman, Los Angeles (Silverlake area)
Street facade remodeled. Interior not inspected.

Residence for H. Wolff, 1938

4000 Sunnyslope Ave., Studio City (corner of Sunnyslope and Contour Dr.) Good condition. Originally designed on a triple lot, the property is today reduced to a single lot. The relationship between the building and the site is therefore lost, and the house's main view is now blocked by the adjacent building. The 'bridge-like' part has also disappeared after the addition of a den on the lower level, filling the original 'tunnel' underneath the house. But the rest of the structure is intact.

Apartment Building for S.T. Falk, 1939–1940

3631 Carnation Ave., Los Angeles (Silverlake area)
Intact. In good condition.

Stores on Ventura Blvd. for W. Lingenbrink, 1939–1942

12634–12670 Ventura Blvd., Studio City
Built in several phases. Altered by signs and awnings, but behind them the facade and its various display windows are still intact.

Apartment Building for P. Mackey, 1939
1137 S. Cochran Ave., Los Angeles
Intact. In good condition. Owned by MAK Center for Art and Architecture.

Residence for A. Van Dekker, 1939–1940
5230 Penfield Ave, corner of Collier St., Los Angeles (Canoga Park area)
Difficult to see from the street.

Residence for G. Droste, 1940
2035 Kenilworth Ave., Los Angeles
Intact. In poor condition on the outside, but the inside was recently restored.

Residence for S. Goodwin, 1940–1941
3807 Reklaw Dr., Studio City
Remodeled. Not much can be seen from the street.

Residence for J. Rodriguez, 1940–1942
1845 Niodrara Dr., Glendale. In good condition.

Three houses on Ellis Ave., c. 1940
423, 429, and 433 Ellis Ave., Inglewood
Some minor remodeling. In good condition.

Residence for J.G. Gold, 1940–1941 and 1945–1946
3785 Reklaw Dr., Los Angeles. Remodeled.

Residence for J. Druckman, 1940–1942
2764 Outpost Dr., Los Angeles (Hollywood Hills area)

Bethlehem Baptist Church, 1944
4900 S. Compton Ave., Los Angeles (South Central area)
In poor condition. Some interior remodeling.

Residence for F. Presburger, 1945–1947
4255 Agnes St., Studio City. Difficult to see from the street.

Residence for R. Roth, 1945
3634 Buena Park Dr., Los Angeles (Hollywood Hills area)
Extensive remodeling.

Residence for F. Daugherty, 1945–1946
4635 Louise Ave., Encino

Residence and Studio for M. Kallis, 1946
3580 Multiview Dr., Studio City
In good condition. The corner terrace that originally linked the two build-

ings has since been enclosed, but in a manner very sympathetic to the original materials and lines of the house.
Visits by appointment only. Call (213) 851–4733.

Residence for R. Lechner, 1946–1948

11600 Amanda Dr., Studio City
Extensive remodeling. The layout has been modified. The terrace between the garage and the house has been enclosed and a triangular staircase added. Only the corner living room with its floating roof plane, detached from the walls, remains intact.

Laurelwood Apartments, 1946–1949

11833-11837 Laurelwood Dr., Studio City
Intact. In good condition.

Residence for E. Janson, 1948–1949

8704 Skyline Dr., Los Angeles (Hollywood Hills area)
Extensive remodeling. Most of the terraces and decks have been enclosed, enlarging the house beyond its original, treehouse-on-stilts appearance.

Residence for A. Tischler, 1949–1950

175 Greenfield Ave., Los Angeles (Westwood)
Intact. In good condition. The upper two-thirds of the blue fiberglass panels of the roof have been doubled with plywood on the inside. The house is still inhabited by its original owners. It was declared an historic cultural monument by the City of Los Angeles in 1991.

Residence for E. Tucker, 1950

8010 Fareholm Dr., Los Angeles (Hollywood Hills area)
Some remodeling.

Residence for M. Ries, 1950–1951

1404 Miller Dr., Los Angeles
Extensive remodeling. Nothing can be seen from the street.

Residence for R. Erlik, 1950–1951

1757 Curson Ave., Los Angeles (Hollywood area)
Extensive remodeling.

Residence for S. Skolnik, 1950–1952

2567 Glendower Ave., Los Angeles
Later additions by Gregory Ain in 1960.

Residence for Schlesinger, 1952

1901 Myra Ave., corner of Franklin Ave., Los Angeles

Photographic acknowledgements:

© Mary Jane O'Donnell/MAK Center for Art and Architecture: p. 31
© Parkett Publishers, Zurich – Frankfurt – New York and the Artists: p. 29
© Julius Shulman: p. 60 (below), 61 (above), 70 (below), 72 (above), 76 (below), 78 (below)
    79 (above), 81 (below, right), 84, 85 (below, left)
© R.M. Schindler Archives, Santa Barbara: Cover, p. 7, 8, 12, 14, 16, 21, 40-43, 45, 50-53, 58,
    59, 60 (above), 62-65, 68, 69, 70 (above), 73, 74, 76 (above), 77, 78 (above), 81, 82,
    85, 86 (above), 91 (left), 93, 98, 100 (above, left, and below), 101, 102 (above)
© Alex Vertikoff: p. 95
© Gerald Zugmann/MAK: p.10, 11, 17, 18, 22, 24, 25, 30, 61 (below), 66, 67, 71, 72 (below),
    75, 79 (below), 80, 83, 88, 90, 94, 99, 102 (below), 103, 104
© Illustrations of the projects by the artists

Graphic Design: Tom Harwerth, Frankfurt/Main, Germany
Cover: April Greiman, Los Angeles
Editing: Jessica Beer, Daniela Zyman, Vienna, Austria
Translations: Catherine Schelbert, Miriam Frank, John Brownjohn

With special thanks to Charles Correa, Jessica Fleischmann, Frank O. Gehry, Philip Johnson,
Tres Parson, Leda Ramos, Michael Rotondi, Judith Sheine, Julie Silliman, Lebbeus Woods
and the Austrian Federal Ministries of Economic Affairs, Education and Cultural Affairs, for
Science, Research and the Arts and of Foreign Affairs.

© Prestel Verlag, Munich and New York
and MAK-Austrian Museum of Applied Arts, Vienna, 1995

All rights reserved.
No part of this publication may be reproduced
in any manner whatsoever without the prior written
permission of Prestel-Verlag.

Prestel books are distributed worldwide.
Please contact your nearest bookseller or write
to either of the following addresses for information
concerning your local distributor.

Prestel-Verlag
Mandlstraße 26, D-80802 Munich, Germany
Tel. (089) 38 17 09-0; Fax. (089) 38 17 09-35
and 16 West 22nd Street, New York, NY 10010, USA
Tel. (212) 6 27-81 99; Fax. (212) 6 27-98 66

Printed in Germany

ISBN 3-7913-1675-3

MAK Governing Committee
Dr. Josef Secky, Austrian Federal Ministry of Science, Research and the Arts
Dr. Rudolf Wran, Austrian Federal Ministry of Education and Cultural Affairs
Mag. Werner Brandstetter, Austrian General Consul in Los Angeles
Peter Noever, Artistic and Executive Director, MAK, Vienna
Daniela Zyman, Curator Special Exhibitions, MAK, Vienna
Robert L. Sweeney, President, Friends of the Schindler House
Harriett Gold, Friends of the Schindler House

MAK Center, L.A. Staff
Mary Jane O'Donnell, Program Director
Robert L. Sweeney, Conservation Curator
Israel Fuentes, Caretaker

Board of Directors, Friends of the Schindler House
Executive Committee
Robert L. Sweeney, President and Secretary,
Harriett Gold, Treasurer
Bettie Wagner, Vice President
John Caldwell, Vice President
James M. Johnson, Vice President

Members
Nancy Sanquist, Eric Schindler, Ian Schindler, Margot Schindler-Ehrens
Judith Sheine, Kathryn Smith

Honorary Members
Michael Bobrow, David Gebhard, Barbara Goldstein, Thomas S. Hines
Stefanos Polyzoides, Emmet Wemple

Honorary Life Member
Bernard Judge

Restoration Consultant
James McElwain

MAK-Austrian Museum of Applied Arts
Stubenring 5, A-1010 Vienna, Austria
phone (43)(1) 711-36-0
fax (43)(1) 713-10-26
Peter Noever, Artistic and Executive Director

We wish to thank the following for support:
Michael Bobrow and Julia Thomas
Dr. Erhard Busek, former Austrian Minister of Education and Cultural Affairs
The Butnik Family
Central Office of Architecture, Los Angeles
Cesar Pelli
City of West Hollywood
College of Environmental Design/Cal Poly Pomona
Dr. Elisabeth Gehrer, Austrian Federal Minister of Education and Cultural Affairs
April Greiman, Design
James Johnson, Architect
Latham & Watkins
Dr. Peter Mahringer, Austrian Federal Ministry of Education and Cultural Affairs
Dr. Christian Prosl, former Austrian General Consul in Los Angeles
Mr. Kurt Rötzer, Austrian Federal Ministry of Education and Cultural Affairs
The Schindler Family
Dr. Rudolf Scholten, Austrian Federal Minister of Science, Research and the Arts

Location of Schindler Buildings in Los Angeles